CIRCLE OF SORROW

CIRCLE OF SORROW

Grieving After Losing a Child to Suicide

Keallie Wozny

RESOURCE *Publications* · Eugene, Oregon

CIRCLE OF SORROW
Grieving After Losing a Child to Suicide

Copyright © 2025 Keallie Wozny. All rights reserved. Except for brief quotations in critical publications or reviews, no part of this book may be reproduced in any manner without prior written permission from the publisher. Write: Permissions, Wipf and Stock Publishers, 199 W. 8th Ave., Suite 3, Eugene, OR 97401.

Resource Publications
An Imprint of Wipf and Stock Publishers
199 W. 8th Ave., Suite 3
Eugene, OR 97401

www.wipfandstock.com

PAPERBACK ISBN: 979-8-3852-5160-5
HARDCOVER ISBN: 979-8-3852-5161-2
EBOOK ISBN: 979-8-3852-5162-9

VERSION NUMBER 07/10/25

Scripture quotations, unless otherwise noted, are from the Holy Bible, New International Version®, NIV®. Copyright © 1973, 1978, 1984, 2011 by Biblica, Inc.™

This book is dedicated to my husband,
with whom I share the grief of losing our youngest son,
and to my personal Circle of Sorrow, those friends who have also
been through the loss of a child, with deep thanks for the many
who gathered around us and wept with us.
This book is also dedicated to the larger Circle of Sorrow,
those many parents I've never met but who know first-hand
the unique grief of losing a child to suicide.
May God give you peace beyond understanding.

CONTENTS

Preface | ix
Acknowledgments | xiii
Endnotes | xv

Chapter 1
THE UNFOLDING | 1

Chapter 2
GRIEF FOG | 28

Chapter 3
ACCEPTING HELP | 41

Chapter 4
GUILT, STIGMA, AND THE UNFORGIVABLE SIN | 58

Chapter 5
MEMORIAL SERVICE | 66

Chapter 6
THE PHYSICAL TOLL | 75

Chapter 7
WHY? | 82

Chapter 8
BELONGINGS | 86

Chapter 9
SIGNS | 93

Chapter 10
MILESTONES | 99

Chapter 11
CHANGES IN RELATIONSHIPS | 113

Chapter 12
WORSHIP, HEAVEN, AND LOOKING AHEAD | 121

EPILOGUE | 134

POSTSCRIPT | 137

Endnotes | 139

PREFACE

Since you've picked up this book, it's likely that you or someone you know has had the unthinkable happen: the loss of a child to suicide. My husband and I lost our youngest when he was thirty-one years old. Loss of a child is unlike any other loss. We needed help. Friends, family, and our church encircled us. And we read. Between us, we read at least twenty books in the first two months. Some books were extremely valuable to both of us; some ministered particularly to one or the other of us; others weren't helpful at all. As we continued to search for practical words of direction and comfort, we discovered that books from a Christian perspective and that speak from first-hand experience with suicide were rare.

After we lost our son, I stayed off social media except for occasional milestone updates posted privately for those who wanted to know how we were doing. At the six-month mark, I posted a somewhat lengthy piece about what we had learned and how people might pray for us. Several people, after reading it, suggested I write a book. Me? The ultra-introvert who lacks the social gene? The pragmatist who believes the fewer words needed the better? Sometimes God uses unexpected people. Even though I doubted it would ever happen, I agreed to pray about it. Suicide needs to be talked about. As Christians, we grieve differently from those who don't have a relationship with the Lord, but God is not a magic genie in the sky who waves a hand and makes everything okay. We grieve with hope, but we still have to go through the long path of pain and searching as we lean on God, day by day, for help, comfort, peace, and wisdom.

This book is a record of and reflection on my experience, written with the hope that it will help someone else as they travel this unwanted path. A few names have been changed for privacy. Some of my husband's thoughts and feelings are also expressed here, with his permission and blessing. We have two surviving children who dearly miss their little brother, but their

Preface

story is their own. Their loss is different, their journey is different, and I have tried hard to respect their privacy. Although they are mentioned in these pages, the details of their grief aren't mine to tell.

As I sat to begin this book, I wanted to write topically rather than chronologically, which means there is overlap here and there. That made sense to me. My own questions were topical: as I moved through layers of grief, I discovered very specific matters I needed to think about and work through. The loss of a child to suicide is very different from losing a child to illness or accident. I'm certain that those parents hurt just as much, but it's still different. Some of what we parents are forced to do under these agonizing circumstances requires looking back over our child's life, trying to understand when it all went sideways and how or whether we could have done anything to change the outcome. For that reason, I feel the need to give more of a life story in the first chapter than would be essential in a book about grief due to a different kind of loss. I think biography is pertinent to this journey through suicide grief, but I realize that for some parents it may be too hard to read. Maybe it's just too soon, or maybe it resonates too strongly. It's okay to skim or to skip sections that are too hard for you. I hope the chapter titles will help those who can't read straight through find what might help.

Six years before we lost our son, a friend lost her five-year-old in a traffic accident. I wept for that family and prayed for them as they mourned the loss of that young life. And then I kept praying for them. I added a few other families I knew who had also lost children, mainly from cancer, to my prayer list. Soon I had five families who I prayed for regularly. Then a friend lost a son to an overdose as he dealt with PTSD. Then another loss to an accident. I asked my friend who lost that last young man how I could pray better for my little group of friends who had lost a child. She asked me to pray that she could sleep. It eluded her. She lay awake nightly missing and mourning her child. Actually, she was missing and mourning the loss of two children, having lost both her sons about twenty years apart. My heart ached for my friends, and I prayed often for the group. Was God somehow preparing me for my own loss as I prayed for this group of people? I don't know, but suddenly we were part of that group, part of a club in which we had no desire to be members. I prayed for us the same things I had already been praying for that group of families. That friend who had lost two children came with her husband to sit with us, and her husband brought us a book, *Seasons of Sorrow*, by Tim Challies. They had not yet read it

Preface

themselves, but they had read enough other books on grief to know that this one was probably a keeper. They were right. Tim Challies and his wife lost a college-aged son to an undetected heart issue. His story is different from ours, yet similar in many ways. About two-thirds of the way through the book, I felt he was describing exactly the place where I was in my own grief. I felt a kinship with him and his wife, as though we were walking side by side through our personal griefs. I found his thoughts honest and filled with hope, even in the face of the sadness he continues to carry. At one point, he refers to an old piece written by Theodore Cuyler in 1868. A minister and writer, Rev. Cuyler lost his three-year-old son to Scarlet Fever, inspiring him to write a booklet, *The Empty Crib: A Memorial for Little Georgie. (with Words of Consolation for Bereaved Parents).*[1] Challies writes,

> It is in the pages of one of Theodore Cuyler's books that I find a comforting phrase. Following the death of his young Georgie, he had received an outpouring of correspondence as so many friends, readers, and parishioners wrote with words of comfort and consolation. He soon came to realize, as have I, that the death of a child had ushered him into 'the sacred circle of the sorrowing,' a community made up of fellow sufferers. He had not been invited into the circle or asked if he wished to join. Rather, Providence had directed him to be part of it, and he had chosen to submit, to bow the knee.[2]

As I read those words, instantly, and with tears, I had a name for my group of families who had lost a child. From that moment on, that group became the Circle of Sorrow. We have a unique bond that none of us wants to have. But we're so grateful not to be alone on this desolate journey.

You are not alone. There are many of us who share this grief. Although it doesn't dampen your pain, there is comfort in knowing there are some who truly understand. Others have walked this road before you, and more will walk it after you. Most of all, you have God, who knows full well what you're experiencing. He, too, lost His Son. Cling to Him, walk with Him, weep to Him as you grieve your indescribable loss.

ACKNOWLEDGMENTS

My prayer team deserves a great deal of credit for this book. Before I wrote a single word, I contacted seven godly women for whom I have deep respect and asked if they would be willing to pray me through this project. All of them said yes. My most urgent need in prayer was for my heart as I reluctantly walked through all the details of that day again. These faithful women understood that, and their prayers and words of encouragement were a comforting quilt wrapped around me. They also kept this book confidential for me. Many people already didn't know what to say to me after losing my son to suicide. I feared that if they knew I was trying to write a book, they might seize that as the perfect topic to bring up whenever they saw me. I didn't want a hundred people at church every Sunday asking me about it, even though it would certainly have been well-meaning. I want my prayer team to know how very much I appreciate their commitment to pray for me. I'm deeply thankful for you, Marilyn Beckley, Ann Budinger, Laurie Chesnutt, Jane French, Valerie Hodges, LaNette Montgomery, and Nan Powlison.

Writing a book is one thing. Having it actually move beyond my own computer is quite another. I'm filled with gratitude that my gifted editor, Marilyn McEntyre, was willing to even read a manuscript from such an unknown. She gave me invaluable insights into using words with care, helped me see my blind spots, and stretched me to present details in more relatable ways. Thank you, Marilyn, and thank you, dear Hank Graeser, for pointing me to her.

I also want to thank the senior pastor at my church, Dr. Steve Constable, who graciously advised me concerning a few theological questions I had lest I lead anyone astray. He is a wise man who has pondered the scriptures deeply and applies them well. He did not, however, examine the entire manuscript, so any incorrect applications of scripture are entirely my fault.

Acknowledgments

Among many others to whom I owe gratitude is Betty Morgan, my alpha reader, who graciously read my edited manuscript and provided me with important feedback. This work improved due to her input. Thank you, dear Betty.

May God use this book to help others who find themselves in the agonizing place of having lost a child to suicide.

ENDNOTES

1. Theodore Cuyler, *The Empty Crib: A Memorial for Little Georgie. (with Words of Consolation for Bereaved Parents)* (New York: R. Carter & Brothers), 102.
2. Tim Challies, *Seasons of Sorrow* (Zondervan, 2023), 128.

Chapter 1

THE UNFOLDING

Steve grabbed two sodas out of the refrigerator and headed out to the back deck beside our youngest child, Trevor. At thirty-one, Trevor towered six feet eight inches tall. He was slender like his dad, and with hair even blonder, the kind of hair women spend a lot of money to attain. After caring all day for my ninety-four-year-old father, in hospice care in our home, I was exhausted and headed to bed, thrilled to see my husband and son sharing some rare time together. Later, I would hear about how they reminisced about old times from Trevor's youth, like the time we came home from a Phillies baseball game late at night to find our garage door open. In that pre-cellphone era, Steve grabbed a bat from the garage and crept stealthily inside, snatching the cordless phone to call the police. The police rebuked him soundly for entering a house where he thought intruders might be lurking. Or the many trips to Peace Valley Park to hike or bike the trails, often ending at the Pooh Tree with its enormous trunk, naturally hollowed out with age to create a house much like the one where A.A. Milne's beloved character, Piglet, lived. Or the first of many backpacking adventures the three guys in the family, Steve, Trevor, and Stephen, older than Trevor by twenty-one months, embarked on. They tackled The Priest on the Appalachian Trail, not realizing they had chosen the most rigorous section of the A.T. in Virginia for their first expedition. Trevor, being only thirteen, felt the impact most and lost his lunch when they finally reached the top. They all agreed the intensity was worth it, even Trevor.

Steve and Trevor sat together on the deck enjoying the warmth of a starlit August evening, laughing and fist bumping repeatedly. Suddenly,

Circle of Sorrow

Trevor turned to his dad and blurted out with distress, "Dad, I don't want to go to hell!"

*

I hope to paint a brief, honest picture of Trevor's life without sugar-coating it. Recalling some of the most pivotal times in his life will provide a broad overview. A book about losing a child to cancer or other disease or to an accident, while just as heartbreaking, may not require the amount of detail included here about Trevor. In the case of a suicide, understanding the backstory is important for making the tragedy even vaguely graspable. What leads up to a suicide rarely happens overnight. It develops over months or years. For that reason, I feel compelled to provide a longer narrative about his life than might be required to understand loss due to other circumstances. I'm not a professional writer. I'm simply a grieving mother, and my prayer, as I put my thoughts into words, has been that God might use my efforts to help somebody else who is going through the unthinkable.

*

Trevor entered the world on a chilly October morning. The largest of my three babies, he weighed in at an even eight pounds, a mop of straight blonde hair plastered to his adorable, wrinkled little face. We quickly discovered his sweet, patient outlook on life as the third child. He cried appropriately to communicate his needs, but when he needed to wait as I tended to the other children and talked to him, telling him he was next, his cries would stop and he'd watch as if he understood my words, shining his precious smile on all of us. I affectionately nicknamed him Smiley Boy, and he continually lived up to it.

One day when he was about a year and a half old, Trevor saw his big brother playing with a little pop-up toy. Stephen found it convenient to place it on top of the kitchen trashcan, exactly the right height for him. Trevor kept an eye on that toy. When Stephen abandoned it, Trevor delightedly carried it into the living room and sat down on the floor to play with it. Shortly afterwards, I told the kids it was time to clean up the toys. Hayley and Stephen, both being a little older, understood the basic concept and began pushing toys into piles and underneath furniture, where they would be out of the way. That was not exactly my idea of cleaning up, but they were little, and I was happy to just have things out from under foot. Trevor, though, picked up the pop-up toy he was playing with and carried it carefully back to the kitchen, placing it gently on top of the trashcan lid where he had found it. He had put it exactly where he thought it belonged. My heart melted as I watched him, thinking, "Oh my goodness I got a neat one!" And that turned out to be true. He got my neat gene, never needing to be told to clean up his room or search the house for a lost library book. He liked things organized and kept them that way on his own.

With two chattery siblings, he didn't say his first word until he was almost two. He probably couldn't get a word in edgewise! I called home from work one night to say good-night to the kids, and Steve told me that Trevor had said his first word. Actually, it was two words. Steve handed him something at the dinner table and Trevor responded, "Take ooo ." How could any mom not love her child's first word being thank you? "Cookie" was his second word the following day, followed by "Amen," and, finally, "Mommy."

At age five, Trevor accepted the Lord Jesus as his Savior. Both of his siblings, Hayley, four years older, and Stephen, had also accepted the Lord at age five. During their college years, all three walked away from Him. Steve and I were heartbroken, but we also didn't want our children pretending they had a faith they truly didn't have. We prayed.

Trevor grew up happy and playful, part of a close group of other homeschooled boys. They dubbed themselves *The Adventure Boys*. Trevor and Stephen put out a monthly magazine with that title as part of their writing assignments, filled with stories, poems, puzzles, and games. They distributed it to friends who subscribed for the hefty fee of zero dollars. They loved all the things typical boys do, and our family enjoyed a closeness as our three children grew and thrived together. For Christmas in 1999, the boys received their first long-wished for guitars. I taught them the basic chords, and they both immediately created music with dexterity and natural skill. Within a week they left me in the dust with my admittedly lame plucking. Steve helped them to play by ear, and the three of them spent hours jamming and learning from each other. For Trevor, music became a source of joy and empowerment. Steve and Stephen steadily progressed in their skills, but both said that Trevor far excelled either of them with an instinctive feel for his instrument.

Employed by a small school for troubled youth, Steve loved his work, but realized that with the typically minuscule salary of a non-public school and no pension, he would never be able to actually retire. In addition, I was asked to cross-train in my job as a Respiratory Therapist and learned Polysomnography, performing sleep studies that required overnight shifts for me. The toll on my body slowly increased, and we began praying about Steve's possibly moving into public school teaching so he might one day retire and I might take a step back from my hours. Unfortunately, in the Philadelphia area every opening for a teaching position received four hundred or more applicants at that time. Steve got to third interviews several times, but eventually we accepted that we would need to relocate. We thought about where we might like to live, and our favorite vacation spot rose to the top of the list. For years, our family had enjoyed summer vacations on a tiny island off the coast of Virginia, with wild ponies roaming free, coves of swans, a lighthouse to climb, dolphins and pelicans bobbing on the waves, and quiet, family-oriented beaches. Steve applied to the Chincoteague Island, VA, school district and landed a job on the mainland, the Eastern Shore of Virginia. Our kids, then ten, twelve, and fourteen, jumped on board with the idea of living on the island, and together we launched into an adventure destined to change each of us in a myriad of unexpected ways.

Ahead of our move I searched online for homeschool groups in our new area. I found only one and connected with the mom in charge. The group differed significantly from what we were used to. Instead of a group of over fifty Christian families and close to two hundred kids, the Eastern Shore group was not only extremely small, but most of the families attended no church and some were not actually even homeschooling. They simply preferred not to send their children to the public schools and to let them learn whatever and however they could manage on their own. Hayley asked to attend public school for the first time in her life, and we agreed. The boys found only one boy close to their age in the homeschool group. He feared being apart from his mother, definitely not an Adventure Boy, and we often got a call from his mother that he preferred not to play after all as our boys watched anxiously through the windows for his arrival. Homeschooling drastically changed as our kids spent substantially less time with peers. We knew there were six churches on the Island but had ruled three out before we moved. We didn't worry, though, knowing that we had three churches to choose from. We visited each of them multiple times and quickly realized with sinking hearts that our beloved vacation spot was not going to be the little Mayberry we had anticipated. The long-time families on the island loved vacationers but resented "come-heres" who settled among them. At the churches, people ignored us as we struggled to find an inroad. We felt unwelcome and rejected and eventually made the difficult decision to attend a church an hour away in Salisbury, MD. We took refuge in the solid theology there, and the kids at the church were very welcoming to ours, but the distance made regular participation in activities challenging. We determined to drive as much as necessary for our kids to be in a good youth group, which quickly embraced all three of them. Yet the distance meant that they were generally not included in spontaneous get-togethers. After a few medical needs arose, we recognized that the care we took for granted near the metropolis of Philadelphia did not even exist in this very rural area. In our opinions, the medical care was sadly substandard. As we settled into our home on the island, disillusionment wore on us. The kids and I made frequent trips back to Bucks County, outside Philly, where we maintained deep friendships from over the years. Families traveled down to visit with us, as well. Those visits back and forth helped to sustain us during three very dry years.

With three years of public-school teaching in Virginia on his resumé, Steve decided to start a new job search. We discussed possible locations as a family, limiting the search to Virginia, since Steve was now in their retirement system. We chose several cities to visit, including Richmond as an afterthought. We looked at real estate and attended a church in each area, and in the end all five of us voted for Richmond. Steve put out applications, landed an interview, and ended up with two offers. He chose a school in Henrico County, and off we forged on another adventure, all of us relieved to depart from that painful season of our lives.

For Hayley, the move meant switching public schools. She transitioned smoothly due in large part to her English teacher, a creative woman and magnificent educator with a gift for bonding with students. As each of the boys reached ninth grade, we asked them to think and pray about whether they preferred to continue to homeschool or to transfer to public school. Both decided to continue with homeschooling, as it enabled them to work part time at Chick-fil-A and also enjoy enough free time to hone their guitar skills. They attended youth group and Sunday School, and nicknames were bestowed upon each of them, signaling acceptance. Stephen became Woz, and Trevor, being smaller, became Wee Woz. As a teenager, Trevor remained his happy, sunny self, but always a quiet kid, not the teen who lit up a room when he entered. The other kids liked him, but he rarely found himself the center of attention, nor did he desire it. He was happy just to belong. He became fast friends with two other boys, and the three of them spent hours at each other's homes and at Pony Pasture, a spot along the James River with huge rocks in the water just begging eager teens to swim out and goof off together.

My intention to return to work once we settled into our new digs disintegrated as my back problems, starting as a young teen, flared up and put me out of commission. A walk to the mail box and back put me over the edge into excruciating pain. I saw specialists and jumped through the required insurance hoops for several years until a doctor reached the end of what he could do for me and referred me to a colleague in a different practice. My new doctor proposed a drastic surgery, feeling certain that without intervention I would be in a wheelchair within ten years. I knew he was being generous in his estimate. I doubted I would last more than two or three years before needing a wheelchair permanently. My recovery would take a full year. Trevor would be the most affected of my children. We discussed doing his final year of high school in the public school system, but he adamantly insisted on sticking with homeschooling. For his senior year, he completed much of his work with only minor oversight by me, but true to his diligent nature, he applied himself, asked when he truly needed help, and successfully finished every course required to graduate.

With the standardized testing we used for homeschooling, we had the option during the high school years to do career testing as well. Hayley, who did hers through her public high school, and Stephen both showed clear career paths, their strengths being dominant in particular areas. Trevor, however, showed possibility all over the graph. Always the kid who performed well in every subject as he grew up, he pondered careers in music, baking, nursing, law enforcement, business, and a variety of other possibilities. Finally, he set his heart on joining the Marines. He enrolled in an early entry program and met regularly with his recruiter while he finished high school. In the summer of 2009, at age eighteen, he set off for boot camp. Halfway through boot camp, he landed in EHP (sick bay) with pneumonia, a common ailment among recruits during the grueling weeks of training. While standing in formation in EHP, as training never ceased even during sickness, he endured fire ants climbing over and into his shoes. Being a good recruit, he controlled every muscle, never flinching and never brushing the brutal insects off. His feet painfully swelled up, and EHP, recognizing a serious problem, transported him to the ER. The ER determined that he was allergic to fire ants, but the doctor there also flagged him for a possible genetic disorder, Marfan Syndrome. He returned to EHP to continue recovering for another month. Then, to his distress, instead of being able to rejoin his platoon, he received a discharge to return home for testing to show he did not have the syndrome, after which he could return to complete boot camp. His dream on the verge of collapse, he glumly boarded the bus to return home, a trip that proved even more agonizing as he rode with the same young men he had labored next to during boot camp, except that they were now Marines, and he was not.

Testing showed that although he had some characteristics of Marfan Syndrome, he did not have the disorder itself. Meanwhile, his feet continued to hurt. The fire ant bites had caused nerve damage that would give him daily pain for the rest of his life. He pushed that to the side, insisting he wanted to return to boot camp. The military promptly lost his records, and even as he persisted, seeking help from his recruiter as well as drill instructors at Parris Island, he slowly became discouraged. We watched as he sank into depression, trying to encourage him, but failing. After two years, he reluctantly concluded that the red tape of the military was an indicator that they would never allow him to return. Working various low-level jobs with no future as he had waited, he now turned to figuring out a different long-term path for himself. He took classes at the local community college and completed an Associate's Degree. He thought nursing might be a good road for him, but abruptly abandoned the thought when we told him that although we had paid for all of his community college and would pay for part of a four-year degree, he also needed to apply for student loans. He decided that he would rather continue in his current job than go into debt. He stopped attending church and his friend group changed. We suspected he was smoking marijuana, more than once detecting its distinctive odor, but he denied it and insisted that the odor came from a co-worker's smoking. He assured us that he knew better than to head down that road.

One night, police pulled him over for a broken tail light as he drove home from his job at an electronics store. He helped unload the warehouse trucks, so he often left work after midnight. Flashing a light through Trevor's car, the officers saw what looked like drugs and asked him to step out of the vehicle. They discovered slightly more than the legally allowed amount of marijuana. Making matters much worse, they also found scales, indicating that Trevor might be dealing. Trevor explained that he and two friends routinely divided up the marijuana they procured using the scales to be fair. Not believing him, the officers convinced him to let them follow him home, to our house, in the middle of the night to search his room, telling him that they could do it that way or they could get a warrant. Clearly not their first time doing such a search, the officers never made a sound. An extremely light sleeper, I never heard them. In Trevor's room, they found a jar containing a suspicious substance which they confiscated for testing. They also found a 9mm Glock, a graduation gift from us to our future Marine. They confiscated that, too. They grilled him for quite some time, finally leaving as quietly as they had arrived.

The next morning, Trevor came clean to us. Stunned, we realized that Trevor's questionable choices had caught up to him. Before long, lab results identified the substance in the jar as cocaine and Trevor was charged. The presence of a gun in his room made it worse. We paid thousands of dollars to hire a lawyer for him with Trevor's promise to pay us back. But even though the large check came from us, we were shut out of any conversations. The charges somehow dropped from a felony to a misdemeanor and Trevor was sentenced to weekends in the local jail for three months. He continued to fight depression. We urged him to seek help, pleading with him that there was no shame in taking some medication to get through hard times. He refused any kind of help. He insisted he was fine and not interested in any kind of medication. He was an adult. We were helpless to do any more than make suggestions.

Not revealed to us at the time, police officers had convinced Trevor to wear a wire. He was small fry. They had determined he truly wasn't selling drugs, but possession was still a serious charge, so they used him for what they needed. They wanted to get to the actual dealer. In order to avoid real prison time, Trevor agreed to wear the wire, thus ending up with a misdemeanor and only weekend jail time. Another young man, identified by the wire Trevor wore, ended up with serious charges and prison time.

Trevor found an apartment and moved out on his own. Whenever we got to see him, he assured us that all was well. His continued depression, though, showed on his countenance, and we worried. He continued to play music, doing gigs at small local spots, and slowly he made headway towards a real career. He chose a job learning French cooking at a local upscale restaurant whose owners had learned their trade in France. He worked from the bottom up.

Around that time, my elderly father decided to take us up on our offer to live with us for his remaining days. Packing up everything he thought he might want, he arrived from Philadelphia driven by my sister, who lives in Richmond as well, and followed by a rented truck of belongings. We got him settled in and proceeded to learn new routines to make this enormous change work for everyone.

One night, Trevor called and asked if he could move back home because he was homeless. Of course, he could! Alarmed, we immediately went and picked him up with some of his belongings and his cat. It turned out he did still have a home, living with two employees from the restaurant, but one had made threats to him and he felt that his past was coming back to haunt him. The young man who had gone to prison because of the wire Trevor had worn had been released, and Trevor sensed word had gotten around that he was a snitch. One of his roommates was friends with some rough people who threatened him with serious harm. Afraid to sleep in the house he rented with his coworkers, he began putting his cat on a leash at night and walked around the streets, sitting with the homeless. He stayed with us for six months, during which he revealed troubled times from his teen years that he had hidden from us, times of being bullied and tormented. He blew up at us one evening about the bad parenting choice of homeschooling that he still struggled with, telling us that we had ruined his life by keeping him from experiencing all the things that public school kids did. My heart wept as I listened. We had tried so hard to parent our children well, pouring ourselves into them, sacrificing more than they ever knew, yet we had failed. We knew that homeschooling meant giving up some things, but it also meant gaining other things. Our kids wouldn't have the experience of multiple teachers and varying viewpoints, pep rallies and school spirit, eating lunch with a dozen friends, finding their way through a large building in time for their next class, going to prom, or struggling with the dreaded rope climb in gym class. The benefits we saw with homeschooling included being able to give each child flexibility to pursue their strongest areas more deeply and being able to work one-on-one with them in their weaker areas. We went with what we thought was the better option. We wished for a do-over, but that obviously couldn't happen, and, without hindsight, we would have made the same decisions. We at least had the sense not to argue with Trevor that evening as he poured out his anger. He didn't want explanations. He wanted to tell us how he felt. We listened, we cried, and we apologized. Later, Trevor and I talked about that evening. I acknowledged that he did miss out on some life experiences by being homeschooled, but I also pointed out that the awkwardness he felt in social situations was more likely due to inheriting my genes, not antisocial exactly, but ultra-introverted. He listened, and appeared to ponder that. Clearly, that wasn't something he could accept quickly, but I was grateful that he would at least think about it. I felt that he needed to see that though homeschooling certainly affected his life, his own personality did too, and he would need to work through that.

After that eruption, Steve and I began questioning every parenting decision we had ever made. Since then, we've spent more hours than I can even begin to keep track of pondering and lamenting that we weren't better parents. Yet even as I continue to think about the many mistakes we made, I believe we did some things right. Our kids were close to each other and to us and had great childhoods until our move to Chincoteague. Even after that, we were a close family. It was during their college years that relationships changed. But that would be a different book. For the purposes of Trevor's story, these details will suffice.

After living with us for six months, Trevor found a new apartment and a new roommate and continued learning the art of French cooking. When he moved out, he accidently left behind a coffee mug, one that he used almost daily, not realizing it was in the dishwasher. When I found it, I held it gently, thinking about Trevor, and decided not to tell him I had it. I put it in the cabinet and began using it regularly, a reminder of my hurting son.

My dad had left his car in Philly and wondered what to do with it. When he heard that Trevor needed a car, he gifted it to his grandson, who rode the train to Philly to retrieve the car.

After that we saw him infrequently. On Christmas 2020 he was sick and stayed away from the family celebration. He withdrew from us, rarely answering his phone and only sometimes responding to texts. By the following Christmas, we had not seen him for the entire year. He stayed away from the festivities again, this time simply because he preferred not to see any of us. Hayley tried to keep lines of communication open with him by regularly creating three-way texts among the siblings, but he rarely responded to them, either. After not seeing him for two Christmases, we made the decision on a freezing January afternoon to wait outside his apartment after his work so we could talk to him for a few minutes and tell him we worried about him and loved him. He came ambling down the street and saw us, two years of Christmas gifts in our hands, and exploded. We had invaded his space. We had ambushed him. We talked, we told him we loved him, we asked how he was doing. It did not go well. He ended up yelling at us as we stood on the sidewalk on Broad Street, livid that we had had the audacity to think we could just show up unannounced and expect him to welcome us with open arms. During that conversation, even in his anger, he told us that he was struggling with continued depression, but because he had no insurance, it was hard to find someone to talk to. After several minutes, as he let himself into his building, I asked him to please just answer texts so I would know he was okay. He answered that he would, and, unexpectedly, added that he loved me, then ducked inside and disappeared. I cried as we left. My sweet boy! None of us had ever imagined his life would turn out like this.

Steve and I returned home and sought counseling from the lay counselors at our church. One couple, Mike and Lisa, specialized in relationships with grown children, having gone through tough times themselves years earlier. We received helpful advice and insights, but when I said I wanted to write Trevor a letter with suggestions and resources, our counselors recommended that we not do that. We prayed and decided that, although their advice was sound, every situation differs. They readily understood. I wrote a letter with contact information for free mental health resources and included a medical discount card, since he had told us he had no health insurance. He had said he wished he could go to cooking school but didn't see any way that could happen. I looked up cooking schools in the area and found one with a flexible schedule for working students. I sent him information about it and offered to pay the tuition. His car needed repairs and we had already volunteered to help him with the necessary funds, so I also included a check. I closed the letter by telling him that I would not bring up any of those subjects again unless he chose to talk about them, in keeping with Mike and Lisa's wise advice. I told him I would respect his decision to talk or not to talk. I mailed it off and knew he had received it when my check was cashed.

I tried hard not to intrude on his privacy. I texted him every few weeks about some mundane thing or other just to be sure he was okay. As promised, he responded, maybe only a word or two, but enough to settle my heart. Months crept by and he continued to miss family gatherings, not even attending his niece's and nephew's birthday parties.

Near the end of July, 2022, Trevor shocked us by texting to ask if his dad could hang out with him that evening. I emailed Steve, our non-texter, at his summer school job to relay the request. Elated, Steve headed to meet Trevor after work, and since they both loved walking, became *Adventure Men*. They explored underneath the A-line Railroad Bridge, a trek known only to other adventurers. They each chose two mementos from alongside the tracks, old discarded railroad spikes. Steve arrived home overflowing with gratitude for time with Trevor, and that Trevor had initiated it. He told me that their conversation largely involved Trevor's confusion over a girl who had broken up with him. Steve noted that Trevor seemed depressed, not unusual for him in recent years. A few days later, Trevor texted again, this time requesting time with me. We ate at a place unfamiliar to me that Trevor loved, and he asked numerous questions about how to manage relationships with girls. He also told me of his newfound art form, graffiti. He showed me pictures and videos on his phone, which I admired for his skill, keeping my mouth shut about the legality of his work. We walked one of his favorite trails through woods, ending at a breathtaking view of the city skyline across a span of the James River. We stood silent, watching the stars just beginning to shine and listening to the pleasant sound of flowing water, finally turning around only because the darkness of the trail might prove treacherous for me.

The following week, Steve received another invitation to spend an evening with him, and then another time for me. That second time for me came on a difficult day with my father. Having been with us for close to three years now, his growing weakness required increasingly more physical help from me. I reluctantly turned Trevor down as my painful body screamed at me to lie down. Steve and I proposed that he join us at our house instead for a chance to say goodbye to his grandfather. He and his grandfather talked, and Trevor gave heartfelt thanks for the gift of my father's car when driving became impossible for the aging man, not mentioning that the car needed so much work it could barely be driven. Trevor sat with us for a few hours, eating and chatting, clearly confused about how to handle some difficult circumstances in his life. We listened intently, but gave him only the advice he asked for, remembering what our counselors had suggested. That sage advice allowed our broken bond to begin to heal. Trevor appreciated that we refrained from bombarding him with unwanted opinions. The next week, I got my second turn to spend time with him. We again picked up food, ate and talked. With a previous nudge from Steve, I broached the sensitive topic of self-harm. I asked my child directly if he ever thought about hurting himself. He paused, then admitted that occasionally he pondered it, but that he had learned that those feelings would pass and he just needed to ride it through. Both alarmed and relieved, I took a deep sigh and silently prayed for wisdom.

The Unfolding

A week later, I missed a meeting with our small group from church. My dad had been hospitalized just after my time with Trevor and returned to our home under hospice care. Being bedridden, He couldn't be left alone in the house. When Steve returned from our small group, he came upstairs to my father's room, where I was reading to him from our current book together. As Steve filled me in on what I had missed at the meeting, I realized that my father was being left out of the conversation. I turned to him hoping to keep him from feeling ignored and asked if he ever thought about Heaven. He said he did sometimes. I told him it would be a good thing to think about, to which he wrinkled his brow and asked, "Why now?" Up until that moment, we had been telling him that he had to regain his strength before he could get out of bed, encouraging him to eat well and keep his spirits up. But now, I revealed the truth to him and answered, "Because, Dad, you're dying!" Tears fractured my voice, and his face registered shock. He collected himself, silently thought for a few moments, then quietly said that we were right, that he did need to think about these things. I asked him what he would say to a holy God if God asked him why He should let him into His holy Heaven. My father reflected and confessed that he had no answer. I shared with him the gospel, that all of us have sinned and therefore cannot enter God's holy Heaven. The wages of sin is death, that is, separation from God. Christ, though, had no sin, so the death He died wasn't payment for His own sin, but for ours. When we stand before God, we have no sin in His eyes, not because we haven't actually sinned, but because Christ's payment wiped out our debt. We can stand before God pure and clean. My father looked at me with clear eyes and said emphatically, "I want that!" He prayed with me, this man who had mocked God for his entire life, and received Jesus as his Savior. In the following days, I read scripture to him, and he stayed awake, listening intently, and told me we should read that every day. This was a change. He normally fell asleep as I sat with him, weak and tired as he slowly declined, but while listening to scripture, he remained completely alert. I sang hymns to him, and he exclaimed over and over how beautiful they were. He was definitely not talking about my voice! He was hearing the lyrics in a way he had never understood them before. Our hearts soared that this man, at age ninety-four and in hospice care, had come to recognize his Creator, literally on his deathbed!

Three days later, on Wednesday, August 24, our landline rang. The caller ID showed Trevor's name. I tried to quell the panic that immediately hit me as I reached for the phone. Trevor almost never called. He texted nearly exclusively. If he did call, he would call my cell phone, not the landline. He spoke quickly in an anguished voice. Someone was searching for him to harm him. Could we come get him? I was stuck, not being able to leave my bedridden father alone. I searched my brain for what friend I might be able to call to sit with my father. My go-to people were unreachable. My father would probably be fine. Did I dare leave him alone? I quickly emailed Steve at school with a 911 in the subject field, explaining Trevor's call and asking how soon he could get to our son, praying that he would see the email immediately. He did. Steve turned his phone on and connected with Trevor, grateful that it was late enough in the day that he was free to leave work, and promptly rushed to his car. On the street in front of Trevor's building, he waited in the car while Trevor ran out with a backpack, raced back for one more bag, then jumped into the car, asking his dad to hurry. He spilled out his observation that someone had been recently following him in a large, black SUV with "super-tinted" windows. Looking back, he frantically declared that he saw the vehicle and urged Steve to exit the highway. Steve saw no such vehicle, but he exited the highway to appease Trevor's distress and drove home via a long roundabout route. Arriving at our house, Trevor gradually grew calmer and we sat down to try to eat. He pushed his food around, nibbling a bit every now and then. He talked about someone trying to hurt him, possibly because of the wire he had worn. We assured him that he was safe right now and we would figure it out. Slowly, he relaxed and became visibly relieved. The guys helped me clean up the kitchen, then I headed upstairs to feed dad and get him ready for bed. When I came back down, Steve had just grabbed two sodas from the refrigerator, and the two of them headed out to the back deck to talk. I headed to bed while they reminisced about old times, laughing and sipping their drinks, until Trevor suddenly turned serious and blurted out, "Dad, I don't want to go to hell."

*

Steve quietly said my name several times and my eyes opened. Something serious must have happened. He would never awaken me, in chronic pain, once I've been able to fall asleep. He leaned over me and told me that Trevor had just come back to the Lord. He had told Steve in anguish that he didn't want to go to hell, and Steve had told him he didn't have to, sharing with Trevor again the gospel he had heard from us since birth. As if hearing it for the first time, Trevor had grasped the message of salvation and held tight. I struggled out of bed, groggily pushing past Steve, and hurried towards Trevor. Gazing into his eyes, I asked him if it was true. He answered yes and I asked him if he had just made his childhood faith his own as an adult. He answered, "I did!" We hugged and I cried tears of uncontainable joy. Two amazing transformations in one week! My dad's eyes were opened on Sunday, and now Trevor's were opened on Wednesday! For years I had prayed that Trevor would return to the Lord and would reconcile with us. Both had happened! Eventually, we all headed to bed, and as we drifted off to sleep, Steve and I marveled over Trevor's renewed profession of faith, giving thanks repeatedly with deep gratitude and joy.

The next morning, Steve left for work for his final two days before students returned the next Monday for the new school year. For teachers, those last few days were crammed to overflowing, unpacking all the things put away for the summer as classrooms received a top-to-bottom scrubbing, with lesson plans, with meetings about new policies, with in-services about new software, and a myriad of other things. Steve would stay at school for as long as possible, trying to get his lengthy checklist completed. I made coffee and noticed Trevor's forgotten coffee mug at the front of the cabinet. I quickly removed it and selfishly hid it away in a desk drawer, wanting to continue to use it once Trevor headed back to his own apartment. I was certain that would happen in a day or two, and I wanted that mug! I loved the reminder of him as I sipped my coffee each morning. That day, as Steve worked, Trevor and I talked. He began unfolding the story behind his fears. He showed me photos and videos of his graffiti, which I admired, again deciding this was not the time to talk about defacing property. He showed me one of which he was particularly proud, his handle, LOP, high up on the top corner of a tall building. It had been so hard to reach, he said, he knew no one would paint over it for a while. He expressed his confusion about a girl who had recently broken up with him for no clear reason. He speculated that she had somehow learned that he was a snitch. He felt that every time he entered a bar, word traveled around the room that a snitch had entered. He wondered if that girl was actually a plant, paid by a gang to get information about him. The young man who had landed in prison because of Trevor's wearing a wire was out, and word was that he was now associated with a gang who could not let a snitch go unpunished. All of this seemed improbable, yet possible. Trevor showed me videos of himself painting graffiti on train cars as they sat unattended in the middle of the night. One section of the train yard, he said, was claimed by a gang. Trevor had ventured in anyway and was warned to stay away. A few days later, he returned and received another firm warning. Now he had crossed the gang. He began noticing the large black SUV following him as he walked in the city. It turned up outside his apartment building and his work. Alarmed, he found himself constantly looking over his shoulder and regretting his choices. I listened as Trevor divulged details about his life that he had not wanted us to know. Among other things, he was looking into growing illegal mushrooms in his apartment, partly for the chronic pain in his feet and partly to relieve his depression. He revealed that he thought he might have mental illness and asked if I thought he had Narcissistic Personality Disorder. I firmly rejected that. I knew some things about that disorder, and it definitely did not fit him: he was sensitive to others, remorseful for his past, and quick to apologize for wrongs. I urged him to see a professional who could give him a diagnosis, and he agreed to think about it. As I cared for my father, Trevor spent hours on his computer trying to self-diagnose and chatting with people on social media platforms. Throughout the day, he asked me to pray with him, and his prayers, heartfelt and sincere, expressed both deep thanks and deep pain. He often asked, "Mom, can I have a hug?" Of course. I treasure the memory of his long, strong arms encasing me. "Mom, can I have a kiss on the cheek?" I knew he was hurting when he asked that, not in character for him. I spent every minute possible with him that Thursday. Sometime in the afternoon, he began lamenting leaving his cats behind at his apartment. His roommate was heading out of town for the weekend, and Trevor worried that his cats wouldn't have enough food. He berated himself for being such a terrible person that he hadn't anticipated they might not be cared for in his absence. As the day wore on, he obsessed over them. I assured him repeatedly that animals notoriously provide for themselves well and that they would be fine. He fretted about his job. He had just received a promotion and was scheduled to start training on French pastries and desserts, his dream position. Certain that he couldn't leave our house safely, he called his boss and resigned. I urged him to wait, to ride this out until he could return to his normal routines in a few days, but he was adamant that he was being disrespectful to his boss, who had been so good to him, if he just kept calling out for work. His boss told him that he would always have a job there, encouraging him to come back when he felt ready. I wept for him in the loss of that promotion, devastated for his crushed dream.

The Unfolding

Steve came home from work and again he and Trevor sat up late talking. Their conversation included none of the happy reminiscing from the night before. Trevor wanted advice. He wanted to untangle the countless complications of his situation. He recounted his graffiti exploits, and Steve listened, as I had, and refrained from criticizing.

Early the next morning, Steve left for work, his last day to prepare for students' return. Trevor, having barely slept for two nights, joined me for coffee. As we talked, he cautioned me that I needed to whisper and asked if we could move upstairs to the loft area at the front of the house with substantial windows. From there, Trevor could see the road clearly, his eyes constantly panning up and down watching for the large black SUV he had seen following him. As he had pondered his situation overnight, he had reached conclusions. He felt that all of our cars had trackers, that our phones were all bugged, and that there were bugs in the house as well. He had decoded the city's recent painting of the bus lanes on Broad Street to red. That was a message, Trevor realized, to him and a few others who had crossed the gangs. It meant, "Blood on the street, blood on the street, you're next!" Trevor went on to describe how the gangs controlled the mayor's office, and if they said paint the lanes red, the lanes would be painted red. It occurred to Trevor that the gang would probably send someone to break into his apartment to plant evidence and then tip off the police. The police, also in the gang's pockets, Trevor said, would come to our house to pick him up, put him in jail for a few hours, then release him, and the gang would be outside, ready to snatch him up. On a private social media message board, someone posted a picture that Trevor believed was directed to him of a man currently being held by a gang in Richmond. Their game with this man was to torture him to the brink of death, bring him back, and then repeat it for years. His narrative changed from the gang wanting to kill him to wanting to capture him to torture him. Trevor looked at me and said, "Mom, they'll make me say things I'll regret, and I'm not strong enough not to." Then he mentioned that our son-in-law would be targeted if they failed to get Trevor. Feeling increasingly alarmed, not knowing how much of what he said was true, I gently told him that I agreed that something was going on with him mentally and we should try to get him seen. He refused. His friends, he said, kept telling him that he was paranoid, but he knew what was actually happening and that his poor decisions were catching up with him. He explained that our house was being watched and that the woods behind the house had secret trails that led all the way out to the main road.

I attempted to visualize those trails. It wasn't possible. There were too many open areas with no place for a secret trail. I decided not to dispute him. My mind spun dizzily. I knew he had worn a wire. It made sense that there would be retribution for that. Interfering with a gang's claimed graffiti area could be a serious infraction. But the red bus lanes and the secret trails through the woods didn't make sense. Again, Trevor asked me innumerable times to pray with him, to hug him, to kiss his cheek. He told me that he loved me and that he knew that everything we had ever done for him, even the things he disagreed with, we had done out of love. He had never known a time, he said, when he didn't know we loved him. I barely held back the tears as my young adult expressed how he had worked through some of the things he had been angry about from his upbringing. I prayed through the morning and afternoon for wisdom and insight, along with much thanksgiving, as I divided my time between caring for my father and sitting with Trevor.

Then the cats came up again. Trevor had asked a friend, the only friend he felt he could trust at that point, to go with him to retrieve the cats. The friend, whom I'll call David, arrived with a shotgun and a pistol for protection, and off they went. I prayed the entire time they were gone. An hour later, they returned with the two cats in tow. David stayed for a while, chatting with Trevor outside so they could smoke. I popped in and out of the house as I worked on a job in the garage that required only a few minutes at a time. They never seemed to change topics when I came out, and their conversation seemed benign. At one point, Trevor went inside and I hugged David and thanked him for being a good friend to Trevor. A little while later, leaving my bedroom, I saw David through the windows driving up the driveway and heard Trevor coming inside. He sauntered upstairs, smiling down at David's shotgun in his hands. I met him at the top of the stairs with a questioning look. It was for protection, he said. I reached for it and he willingly handed it to me. I said, "How about we just keep that in here?" as I went back into the master bedroom. Trevor immediately accepted the confiscation. I knew that he had learned that if he felt like hurting himself, he could ride it out. Even with the uneasiness I felt, his quickly releasing the weapon to me suggested my worries were unjustified.

The cats, both rescues, now took up our focus. The larger cat, Bill, marked every room in the house except the master bedroom, since I had closed the door, and my father's room within five minutes of arriving. Oh, what a stinky cat! The other cat, his new rescue, Phasma, refused to exit her

The Unfolding

carry crate. Trevor put food and water outside the open door, but for hours, she huddled fearfully in the back of the crate. Never having owned a cat, I knew nothing about them. Phasma's fear apparently stemmed from abuse by a former owner. She feared everyone and everything. Several hours later, we noticed she had disappeared. After an extensive search with flashlights, we discovered her under a low piece of furniture in the next room. She emerged only to eat and drink and use the litter box, and only when the coast was clear of people and the other cat.

I made dinner, fed my father, and sat with Trevor, talking about his worries until Steve came home. He had stayed at school preparing until the last possible moment, arriving home, exhausted, after 9:00 that evening. "You need to whisper," Trevor insisted. He told how he and David had gone for his cats, guns in the air. I mentioned to Steve that David had left his shotgun with Trevor and that it was in our bedroom. Trevor recounted many of the things about this gang he had told me during the day. Steve, sensing as I had that much of what Trevor thought couldn't be true, tried to bring him to that recognition. Trevor remained unyielding, adding more details to convince his dad. Steve steadfastly continued to plea with our boy to try to see the flaws in his logic, his own frustration mounting as he tried unsuccessfully to get through to him. In an attempt to jump in before an argument started that would cause Trevor to lose the trust he had finally placed in us, I asked Steve to pause and just listen for a few minutes, trying to put himself in Trevor's shoes. Steve started, suddenly realizing that his own weariness from his long day had kept him from actually engaging deeply with Trevor. He had wanted a quick conversation followed by some dinner. He mentally released his own desires and sat back, looked Trevor in the eyes and asked him to tell him what was going on. The fears of the gang who was after him poured out. Steve suggested calling the police, but of course, Trevor would have none of that. If the police came, they were in the gang's pocket, Trevor told us, and would arrest him for any crime they dreamt up in order to release him then to the gang. When Trevor finally ran out of words, Steve quietly gazed at him in silence, his entire countenance changed. He suddenly shared Trevor's fear. He told us that as part of the final day before students returned, the teachers had attended an in-service about gang activity in Richmond. It was serious, the speaker said, and it was in the schools. The teachers listened for nearly an hour to information about gang related clothing, signs, tattoos, graffiti, and much more. The two big-name gangs that most people have heard of had arrived in Richmond, as well as numerous smaller gangs. Much of what Trevor said rang true to what Steve had heard at the in-service. The three of us sat, pondering. We prayed. We asked for wisdom and guidance. Steve declared, in the required whisper, that we needed to get Trevor far away. Trevor shot that down, certain there would be no place he could hide. Steve proposed a plan. "Look," he said, "we know a retired army Colonel, a ranger. He's done extractions. He could get you someplace safe." Trevor looked at his dad and asked, "Do you like your friend?" "Of course," Steve answered. Trevor questioned, "Is he married? Does he have children? Because if you get this friend involved, they'll be killed." Steve was deflated and frustrated, but offered another plan. "We know a woman who knows people in high places. She's worked for three presidents. She could get you a passport instantly. We have connections in Scotland, people who would take you in immediately." While this was not made up, we had no idea if our friend could actually get him an instant passport, but Steve's true goal was to just get Trevor into the car and take him straight to an ER. Again, Trevor posed the same questions: "Do you like your friend? Is she married? Does she have children?" He reiterated that "they" were watching the house and would stop any attempt to leave. We whispered until well past midnight and finally agreed that we all needed to try to get some sleep. I reminded Steve that the shotgun was in our bedroom as I headed up before the guys. My own firearms were well hidden in lock boxes, ammo and keys hidden separately. I had no way to lock up David's shotgun, but I did have a steel security bar, purchased during the 2020 demonstrations in Richmond when the violence threatened to move to the suburbs. The bar wedges underneath the doorknob. Strong intruders would be able to get past it, but at least they'd be slowed down so I could get to my firearms. After Steve came up, I placed the security bar under the doorknob so Trevor couldn't quietly come in for the shotgun while we were sleeping. I slept fitfully, but Steve, utterly exhausted, went into an immediate solid slumber.

At 7:00 on Saturday morning, Trevor tapped on our bedroom door. Steve slept through it, but I quickly got up and grabbed my bathrobe, not stopping to even brush my teeth. I slipped into the hallway and whispered that dad needed to sleep a little longer. I always guarded Steve's Saturday morning sleep, the only day he gets to catch up on the rest he needs. Trevor and I made coffee and sat upstairs in the loft area again, keeping a close eye on the street. Trevor's face revealed that he had gotten little sleep. We prayed and talked, and I tried to allay his fears. He sighed and said he wished he could see Brad, a young man from church a few years older than he who had always been kind to Trevor. I knew that if I texted Brad, he'd be at our house in a heartbeat, probably with his brother, Joe, in tow. I also knew that Trevor would explode that I had put Brad and his family in "danger." I wanted to call our other children, but again, Trevor feared that our phones were bugged and calls to anyone would put them in harm's way. Trevor told me that if he didn't spill his own blood before the gang got to him, they'd kill me and his dad in front of him and then still kill him, too, or capture and torture him. Trying hard to hide my panic as I listened to his thoughts, I tried to get him to see that he was not understanding the situation clearly, but his paranoia seemed to be increasing rapidly. I held off until 8:30 and then tiptoed in to wake Steve up. I told him that his son needed him. Instantly wide awake, he quickly dressed and rushed out to Trevor. As the two went downstairs for more coffee, I grabbed the first clothes I found and pulled them on. My father generally slept until I awakened him, his aged body weary. I peeked in and, relieved to see him sound asleep, hurried downstairs. Again, coffee in hands, we all returned to the loft so Trevor could watch the street. For an hour, we whispered and continued to pose possible options, all of which Trevor refused. He told us more details of various friends and his suspicions that they were actually being paid by the gang to give information about him. He told us that he had hundreds of cans of spray paint in his bedroom, and if the gang tipped off the police, they'd come arrest him for his graffiti. With an empty cup, Steve excused himself to brew some more coffee. Moments later, footsteps sounded down the hallway, the front door opened, and Steve appeared outside, walking quickly up the driveway. Trevor and I looked at each other in bewilderment. I shrugged and said I guessed he needed his normal morning walk, though I doubted that was what was going on. Fifteen minutes later, Steve returned, ambling slowly down the driveway. He came inside and rejoined us in the loft. Trevor and I gazed at him questioningly, and he told us he had just needed some fresh air. Five minutes later, a red pickup truck pulled up in front of our house and parked. We have a deep half-acre front yard, lined with trees and shrubs along the top, but the vehicle was clearly visible. Trevor, on high alert, said, "They're here!" We assured him that local landscapers and lawn care companies parked out there all the time. This was true, but without the usual utility trailer we doubted that this pickup was there for anyone's lawn. Trevor paced, never letting his eyes leave the pickup. Steve told him he would go out and pretend to check the mail and figure out who was out there. Frantic, Trevor implored him to stay inside. "Dad," he pleaded, "you can't do that! They'll kill you!" As we watched, a second vehicle pulled up next to the red pickup. Trevor recognized it immediately, a large black SUV with super-tinted windows. It blocked the road. Our cul-de-sac was cut off. There was no in and no out. We heard Trevor say, "That's it. It's time." Steve yelled at him to get in the car, that he would get them out of there. "You can't, Dad." Steve argued, but we all knew that with the ditches on each side of the vehicles blocking the road, we were trapped.

"It's time," Trevor stated again. I cried out with distress, "No, it's not time until someone is coming down the driveway! It's NOT TIME!" I was certain no one was going to come down the driveway. I had to delay him. Steve looked at us both in confusion. Trevor headed towards our bedroom, but not as fast as I did, blocking the door with my body. Steve, realizing that Trevor intended to harm himself, rushed over and tried to speak logically to his distraught son. "Trevor, how are you going to harm yourself? It's not like you have a gun. What are you going to do? Do you have poison?" I looked at him in confusion and reminded him that David had left his shotgun with Trevor, that it was in our bedroom. That fact had completely flown past Steve. He had had so much swirling in his head when I had told him, that it simply hadn't registered. Time was ticking. Trevor put his hands on my shoulders and gently shifted me out of the way. Looking back, I weep every time I remember how gentle he was, even in his panic, knowing that with my back problems he could hurt me with a wrong movement. Steve grabbed him, but Trevor wrestled away and slammed our bedroom door, locked it, saw the security bar, and jammed it under the doorknob. Steve pounded and kicked at the door. "Call 911," he yelled to me, and to Trevor, "You'll break your mother's heart!" I raced down the stairs as I dialed 911. I knew, of course, that Trevor was just getting his breath and thinking, that he wasn't going to take any actual action, but I didn't want him to panic if he heard me calling the police whom he feared. Yet even as I tried to convince myself that it wouldn't happen, terror exploded inside me as I faced reality. I raced in a circle through the downstairs, answering the 911 operator.

"What is the address of your emergency?"

I stated each digit of our house number loudly and carefully, plus the street name, enunciating as clearly as I could so as to not waste a second, followed by city, state, and zip code.

"Please repeat the address."

Infuriated, I tried to stay calm as I loudly repeated the information, as clearly as I could.

"What is the nature of your emergency?"

"Our son is trying to take his life! Please send help!" As I stated my plea, the shot went off. I screamed into the phone, nearly hysterical, "NO, NO, NO, he did it, send help, send help, please send help!" Running back up the stairs, horrified, I reached the top just as Steve finally got the door kicked in. He ran in, then ran back out. He saw enough to know there was nothing he could do. He somehow knew that he shouldn't see any more. The 911 operator told me to go in and see if CPR was possible. I entered and told her, now fully hysterical, that it was not. She asked me to describe how I knew it was not possible. In seven wrenching words I described the scene, words that will never cross my lips to another human again. No one should try to imagine those words. No one needs to know them. No one needs to have them in his or her memory. She directed us to leave the house and wait outside for the police, which we did. The red pickup and SUV were gone. As we sat on the front porch steps, we wailed unlike any wail that either of us had ever experienced. Deep, guttural, agonizing pain poured out of our mouths. We sat, gripping each other's hands, praying, asking God, our Anchor, to hold us fast. "We don't understand," we cried to God, "but we know that You're wise, that You're loving, that You're fully in control. Lord, we don't know what to do. We don't know how to do this. Help us, Lord." The 911 operator stayed on the line with us until police officers arrived, twelve minutes after I had placed the call. We began the excruciating process of relaying all the details to the police. They took notes and explained what the procedure would be. An ambulance pulled in. An officer asked if there was anyone we could call. Our pastor, we thought. No, our senior pastor was out of the country. The youth pastor, though, knew Trevor and knew us. Yes, we needed Zac. I attempted to scroll to the C's on my phone, but my fingers had forgotten how to scroll. I handed my phone to the officer, told him "Zac Collins," and the officer took it from there. Zac came immediately. He sat with us, wept with us, prayed with us, and stepped in to take care of things we were in no condition to do. He asked if there was anyone he could call for us. "My dad," I told him. "He hasn't even had breakfast. Can you call my sister?" Zac placed the call and explained to my sister what had happened. Although she had a full-time job, she regularly spent as much time at our house with our dad as she was able and was familiar with his routines. She arrived, hugging us and crying with us, then headed in to take care of our father, removing that weight, suddenly so tiny, from my shoulders. Although awake now, without his hearing aids he was oblivious to the activity outside his bedroom door. Various officers requested all the details several times, some hearing backstory, some not. Reliving the past ten years, the past year, the past month, the past hour over and over as we sat on the steps, the ironically glorious sun shining down on us, we cried more intensely than we knew was possible. "Oh Lord, we know You'll never leave us or forsake us. We need you. Oh Lord, help us!" Someone brought a box of tissues. Appropriately banished temporarily from our home, we sat, the scene we had witnessed, the sound of the gunshot, the odor of the gunpowder still drifting out every time the storm door was opened, flooding every cell in our bodies. The pile of tissues next to me grew, spilling over the edge of the porch, soggy white weeds in my garden. I recalled a Ugandan preacher from years ago speaking about how at times, we possess no words for the pain we feel, and at those times, all we can do is cry out the name of Jesus. "Jesus, Jesus, Jeeeeesuuuuus!" We gasped out our Lord's name, over and over. A police officer told us we needed to find a trauma scene cleanup company. Zac instantly took that task, finding a company who could assess the job that evening. He also contacted a couple we knew who had lost a child to cancer some years before, a different type of loss, but still the loss of a beloved adult child. Already friends, Butch and Judy would be an appropriate help and comfort to us.

Steve finally got to tell me where he had gone when he had rushed out the door as Trevor and I had watched. He had secretly called 911. The police said they would come, but Steve implored them not to. He just wanted advice. Protocol, though, said that they had to respond. Steve begged them not to come to the house, which would panic Trevor, and asked if he could meet them at the top of our street. The police agreed to that, and Steve rushed off. Before long, six police cars sat on the cross street. They listened sympathetically, then spelled out the laws in place to protect citizens. There was nothing they could do unless something actually happened. They asked if Trevor had any weapons. Steve assured them that he did not. The officers told him that he could get a form signed by a judge over at the courthouse that would allow them to transport Trevor to an ER. Exasperated, Steve walked slowly back to the house, praying the whole way. It was Saturday. The courthouse was closed. Even if it was open, this urgent situation didn't have a window for waiting at the courthouse for a possible signature. He carefully forced a change to his countenance as he ambled down the driveway as though he had simply gone out for a morning walk. And five minutes later, the red pickup arrived. As Steve relayed his initial 911 call, the two vehicles that had pulled up in front of our house suddenly began to make sense. We realized that people listen to police scanners. If they live nearby something intriguing they hear about, they go to watch the "excitement." Those two vehicles had almost certainly been looky-loos or reporters, trying to see firsthand what others would hear about only later. The second pulled up beside the first so they could share notes. The similarity of the SUV to the one Trevor felt had been following him was just a horrible coincidence. As we talked through the likelihood of those vehicles truly belonging to gang members, recalling the many things that Trevor had feared that clearly couldn't be true, it became plain to us that those people were simply trying to see the news story first. The drivers of those two vehicles will never know what their mere presence galvanized that morning. And now the same officers who had met with Steve at the top of our street were inside our home, tending to the horrible ending they had not been able to help us avoid.

We remained on the porch, praying and sobbing, "Oh Lord, help us, hold us, meet us!" Police kept us informed about the status of their process and allowed us to ask questions. Relaying what Trevor had told us about gangs holding people to torture over and over, we wanted to know if that was true. The officer said that it was, that it was happening in Richmond right now. He asked which gang our son had crossed. I knew the name, not one that I had ever heard before, but was afraid to tell him. Maybe there really were bugs in the house! Trevor had specifically mentioned our son-in-law as a possible target because of him. I was terrified that I might put our son-in-law in danger by telling the name of the gang. Even if the house wasn't bugged, did the police and gangs have communications as Trevor had thought? Would the police leak to that gang that I had named them? No, I couldn't tell them the specific gang Trevor had mentioned.

We asked that we be alerted before our son's precious body would be removed from the house. We didn't want to see him taken out on a stretcher, covered completely, another vision we would never be able to erase from our minds. They relocated us to our back deck. Butch and Judy arrived laden with necessities. Other people arrived as well, and my brain has only cloudy memories of the activity in our kitchen. I remember Judy and Gayle unloading basics like bread, peanut butter, paper towels, toilet paper, and paper plates. "Paper plates?" I wondered. "Why paper plates?" No matter,

I trusted that Judy knew what she was doing. She and Gayle planned to clean the bathroom. I remember telling them in a daze that I had cleaned it a few days before, that it was okay. They quickly abandoned that plan, not because they weren't willing, but because they were being extremely gentle with me, wanting only to help and not insert themselves in any way that might seem intrusive. Lynn, our church's office administrator, arrived with more groceries, and flowers appeared on our kitchen table. She asked if we wanted meals. I was being asked to make a decision, a power I sadly lacked at that point. Lynn understood. I shrugged helplessly and answered, "I don't know." I didn't understand at the time, but I was beginning to learn what being in shock feels like. As we sat on the deck, a new pile of tissues continually expanding, Zac received a phone call from his wife. Another death, another tragedy. He was needed elsewhere. He chose to stay with us for a while longer. Another call came about the same tragedy. We urged him to go as Butch and Judy assured him and us that they intended to stay for as long as needed. Our already-high respect for Zac skyrocketed that day.

We knew we had to contact our other children. Our daughter was working that Saturday. I texted her to call me when she left work. Our other son lived in another time zone and was also working, so I delayed texting him until closer to the end of his shift. Hayley's shift ended, but she didn't call. I stared at my phone, resting in my lap, willing her to call. No call came. Dusk approached, the police completed their work, and we moved into the living room. An hour after she had left work, Hayley finally called. I asked her to go someplace private in her house, away from the kids. She confirmed that she was away from the kids and asked if her grandfather had passed away. Her delay in calling immediately made sense. She had said her goodbyes; she knew that he was in hospice care and would pass away soon. She wanted to get home before coming alongside me in that loss, to be unrushed. I had not thought through how to tell her. I gulped. I told her, "Honey, Trevor called us on Wednesday. He thought someone was after him." I stopped, my throat constricted, unable to breathe. "Honey," I got out. I tried to choke out more. Hayley, fear in her voice, said, "Mom?" I tried again. "He. . .he. . .he," I fumbled, not able to say the actual words. "He told us a lot of things," I said instead. Again, I had to stop. I could barely breathe. I couldn't say the words. It would be the first time I had said the nightmarish truth out loud. Hayley, audibly on the verge of tears, said, "Mom, you're scaring me!" I had to just say it. "Honey, he took his life." We both broke down with heaving sobs. "Mom, I'm on my way." Steve and I wept anew as we thought of Hayley and Stephen losing their brother. I tried to collect myself to be able to text Stephen. I couldn't see my phone and sat, crying, crying, crying. Finally, I texted him with the same message I had sent Hayley, to call me when he left work. He called immediately. In a pained voice, he told us Hayley had already reached him and he was working on getting plane tickets. He would arrive the next day.

An hour later, Hayley arrived laden with what we didn't know were essentials. How did she know? I will be grateful forever! She brought weighted blankets and an over-the-counter sleep medication. She brought healthy individually wrapped breakfast foods and snacks appropriate to leave on the table for those times when we knew we needed to eat, even though our appetites had disappeared. I can't even remember what else she brought, her arms barely able to carry it all. I'm pretty sure she thought of tissues and other basic food items, but my mind is blurry on much of what went on right after The Event.

Long after dark everyone trickled out, leaving us alone for the first time since it had happened. We picked at a little food, mostly unsuccessfully. Two or three bites overfilled our stomachs. We sat in our living room, side by side, holding hands and weeping. Our boy, our beautiful boy! Our sparse conversation alternated with frequent prayers. Gasping out the words through my tears, I voiced what we both already knew, that there were going to be times as we moved through this horror that one of us would want to talk and the other didn't, and that we both needed to do our best to respect the other's needs. Steve suggested that we put on a movie, some old classic or other that we had seen multiple times. I prepared my new bed, the sofa, and Steve unrolled his sleeping bag nearby. I gratefully took some of the sleeping medication that Hayley had brought and lay down under the weighted blanket she had also provided. The movie proved to be exactly what we needed to distract us without requiring us to actually pay attention. With a damp pillow and a box of tissues on the floor next to me, I somehow drifted off to sleep not too far into the movie.

Chapter 2

GRIEF FOG

We sat on the front porch after The Event as Zac read scripture and prayed with us, interspersing those with gentle talk about practical matters that required attention and decision. Zac has experienced deep loss in his own life, and as our youth pastor, has also helped teens through some difficult deaths of friends at the local high school. He knows grief. As he sat with us, he leaned in, looking steadfastly into our eyes. "There's something called grief fog," he told us, "and it's real." In the days and weeks that followed, that sentence returned to my thoughts repeatedly as I experienced the strange disorientation of grief fog. I wondered if Zac knew how meaningful those factual words would be as Steve and I both felt as if we were in a constant trance. It helped enormously to know that what we were experiencing was normal in grief. We performed the daily things that required doing, plodding slowly through the house, shaking our heads occasionally as if the cobwebs would evaporate and we'd wake up from this ghastly nightmare. The nightmare remained.

On the second day, Sunday, I woke up too early, still in the clothes hastily pulled on the day before. I lay in the dark, shifting restlessly, and Steve whispered, "Are you awake, too?" We resigned ourselves to getting no more sleep and got up. As we sat together at the kitchen table, weeping over coffee, trying to eat something, I realized why Judy had brought paper plates. I had no energy to empty the dishwasher, and certainly no energy to fill it back up again. What a wise and practical gift those paper plates were. Over the next month, others who brought meals thought of the same thing, and we gratefully had little cleanup to do each day. Grief is exhausting. For the first several months, I often slept for ten to twelve hours a night. Steve was provided with a long-term substitute teacher for his classes, and his principal stayed in touch with him but put no pressure on him to return before he felt ready.

Our son Stephen arrived on Sunday afternoon. We had already discussed with Hayley the need to make funeral arrangements, and when she arrived, she had researched cemeteries in our area with locations, contact information, and pricing. As we all looked at the loathsome information, Hayley and Stephen respectfully held back their opinions, allowing Steve and me to contemplate the possibilities. We agreed that Hollywood Cemetery seemed like the most beautiful and peaceful of the choices. An attractive, historic cemetery in Richmond, where five U.S. presidents as well as numerous other people of note are buried, it's well-maintained and is designed for walking, with paved pathways throughout. Hayley said she had hoped we would choose Hollywood, as she already often walked there. Together, we drove to look at plots. How could that be? We were looking for a cemetery plot for our child! Trying to maintain a morsel of composure, we trudged behind the director as he led us to a number of possible sites where we could bury our son and later be buried next to him ourselves. As we toured the massive property, Steve gazed at the thousands of headstones and pondered aloud the families who had already laid loved ones to rest, followed by themselves, their children, their grandchildren, and their great-grandchildren. A strange peace came over him, the first peace since The Event, as he reflected on the brevity of our lives here on this earth and the anticipation of eternity with our Lord after that. We close plots for Trevor and ourselves under a maple tree, directly in front of two aged graves with full slab markers engraved with beautiful scriptures. We would make sure that our own markers were low enough so as not to obscure those precious words only feet away.

Still in a fog, we spent a few days with our other children, talking about everything and nothing, trying to make sense of what had happened, and especially wondering if the rest of us, particularly our son-in-law, were in danger. We realized we needed to retrieve Trevor's basic belongings from his apartment. We knew his former girlfriend's first name. Hayley, an able internet sleuth, found a full name and contact information. She reached Anna-Mae, (don't mess with a southern girl's hyphenated name! It's Anna-Mae, never ever Anna!), who confirmed she could let us into Trevor's apartment. Gathering boxes and packing tape, we all headed into the city.

Anna-Mae met us there and let us know that Trevor's roommate was home. He let us in, and both helped for a short time to identify what belonged to Trevor and what belonged to the roommate. Hayley asked for privacy for the family, and they both graciously left us alone. In a stupor, we blindly dumped precious belongings into boxes, a too-short lifetime of mementos jumbled into unorganized heaps and sealed shut. We left the furniture and kitchenware for the roommate to continue to use. As I packed, I repeatedly reexamined each room, mystified, searching for the hundreds of cans of spray paint that Trevor had been fearful the police would find, bewildered that none surfaced. There was no spray paint, none at all. I found spray paint can nozzles and a paint-spattered bag he apparently used to carry his cans when he went out to create graffiti, but not a single can of spray paint. Did they put it in David's car when they retrieved the cats? Did the roommate move it, knowing that Trevor was afraid it would be found? I peeked into the roommate's bedroom and saw only a few cans of paint in a small box. Also a graffiti artist, that was to be expected. I tucked that mystery away to ponder later.

Hayley, her husband, and Stephen headed off with full cars to unload into our garage. As Steve and I prepared to place the final boxes into my car, I noticed a large black SUV with super-tinted windows parked across the street. Alarmed, my eyes darted around in every direction, but nothing seemed amiss. The benign-looking car appeared to be simply parked there, with no one visible from where I stood. Was that the car Trevor had been so fearful of? Had he seen it and in his mind created a paranoid scenario from the innocent parking of a local resident's vehicle? If that vehicle had truly been following Trevor, there was no need for it to be here any longer. The driver would have known what had happened. Even in my fog, I realized it belonged to somebody who happened to live across the street from Trevor. The lingering doubts in my mind trickled away. Yes, those two vehicles had certainly been curious looky-loos.

At that moment, Anna-Mae burst out of the apartment building, crying hysterically. Running to us, she sobbed, "I didn't know! I didn't know!" Hayley had not been able to explain to Anna-Mae why we were emptying Trevor's apartment. I fully understood why she hadn't. Uttering the actual words that he had taken his life gave an unchangeable finality to the situation that none of us wanted to accept, and speaking those words to a stranger would twist the dagger already in our hearts. We gathered Anna-Mae into our arms, the three of us wrapped together on the sidewalk on

Grief Fog

Broad Street, wailing loudly, our shoulders damp with each other's tears, oblivious to the busy traffic and pedestrians hurrying past. Anna-Mae told us that Trevor was the love of her life. As we all finally gulped for air and regained our composure, albeit poorly, we exchanged contact information and promised to stay in touch.

Returning home, we all unloaded Trevor's belongings into our garage, with some spilling over into the dining room. Emotionally gutted, we at least had the relief that the horrendous task of retrieving them was behind us. The next day, we got a call from Trevor's roommate. He was moving back to New York. He couldn't stay. He needed a fresh start, and the landlord wanted the apartment, which was in Trevor's name, emptied immediately. Steve called Butch in a panic, who arrived with his pickup truck and another strong man. While I remained with my dad, the three of them headed back downtown. They loaded up furniture and put what didn't fit beside a dumpster nearby. Those items would no doubt be given new homes by local people. They would never know why those precious pieces had been discarded. A few hours later, every room in our downstairs contained boxes, furniture, and plants, all piled haphazardly wherever they landed. We had no energy to organize. It would be weeks before we slowly rearranged the unopened boxes and furniture to at least be able to move around the house more easily.

The professional trauma cleanup crew arrived early in the week. It would take five days to complete their task. The three young men who comprised the team treated us with great respect and sensitivity. We asked Luke, the supervisor of the team, if he could get some things from our bedroom for us. He quickly retrieved some essentials for us, mostly hygiene items. For the first week, my daily goal was to brush my teeth and eat something. Although I reached that goal, I accomplished little else. The days passed, but looking back, I have no idea how I spent the time each day. I felt as though a cloud had encompassed my brain, and often it sent a rainstorm that poured out through my eyes. In his blog post from September 3, 2022, David Huffstutler describes his grief fog following the loss of his wife four months earlier.

> The atmosphere, around my head and my heart, has been so scattered and non-focused. Much like looking through a camera lens that's pulled all the way back, the image of our daily life is blurred. . . though a picture can still be snapped, the clarity to understand what's really going on is absent. That's what the fog of

grief is at the moment, there is so much to handle/process/navigate and such a lack of focus/clarity on the roadmap that it creates this general sense of life moving forward and I haven't the slightest idea around anything else. What an opportunity to trust that the Lord is establishing my steps (even in the absence of an unclear way planned on my end) [Prov. 16:9].[1]

I understand better what Job meant when he said "My eyes have grown dim with grief; my whole frame is but a shadow" (Job 17:7). I plodded around our house, one foot in front of the other, forgetting why I had gotten up, circling back to fall into my chair again. Steve and I talked and also sat silently for hours. We tortured ourselves brooding on what we could have done differently. We mulled over every detail, agonizing that when we had realized the severity of Trevor's mental illness, we had been helpless to find a way to get him to someone who could intervene. I dwelt on not hiding the shotgun more thoroughly. Steve exclaimed that had he known the gun was there, he would have broken it in pieces and thrown it into the woods. He said it had never registered with him when I told him it was there. He even slept right over it. It was as if, he said, some strange force had prevented him from hearing it was in the house. He was quick to tell me that he was not blaming me, and our counselors and some friends with experience with mental illness later affirmed our thought that if he hadn't succeeded in ending his life right then, it still would have happened. I wept again just thinking about my boy doing the horrible act alone in his apartment or someplace else, where a stranger would find him, or worse, a friend or his roommate. I had a strange glimmer of thankfulness that he had come to us, the one place he knew he was completely loved. The memory of The Event haunts me, but how dreadful it would have been for another young person to have found him and to have that memory for the rest of their lives. I gave unanticipated thanks that it had happened at our house.

I knew I needed to tell David. I could see missed calls from him on Trevor's phone, even though it was locked. I contacted the mother of the friend who had introduced Trevor and David, and she had his number. I texted him, but as my number was only one digit different from Trevor's, David thought I was Trevor. I asked him to call me. He did, cheerfully greeting his friend, only to hear me instead. I told him that I needed to tell him something. He became serious, but obviously had no idea what was coming. I told him quietly and with no details that Trevor had taken his life. David, stunned, just uttered statements of disbelief, repeatedly. I didn't tell him how it had happened, and he didn't ask. I was sure that if he didn't immediately realize it, he would later think about the shotgun he had provided and know that he had inadvertently had a part in Trevor's action. I haven't spoken to him since, and as far as I know, he didn't come to the memorial service, but I bear him no ill will. I don't blame him in the slightest. He was simply trying to be a good friend. The police took the weapon, and I'm sure they traced the serial number, so perhaps they contacted him. I don't know or need to know, but my heart aches for David that he has to live with knowing he provided the firearm that ended his friend's life.

Two well-meaning people immediately urged us to move. We knew they loved us, and Steve and I agreed we should discuss that option. We concluded quickly that this wasn't the time to make such a major decision. I was familiar with the studies done over the years about making major life decisions in the aftermath of a tragedy or trauma. Jill Cohen, a nationally recognized grief counselor, addressed this in an article on her website:

> The phrase "don't make any big decisions for the first year after a loved one dies" is not a myth. It's a rule, and there are good reasons for it.
>
> The death of a loved one is, for sure, one of the most stressful events a person can endure in a lifetime. Whether it is unexpected or expected, it is still a shock to your system and makes even the tiniest of tasks and minor decision-making very difficult.
>
> . . .Four of the "big ones" where the "no big decisions for the first year" rule applies. . .
> Moving.
> Ay, stop right there.
> For many, the initial response to a death is: I have to move.
> It is suggested that you delay this life event for at least six months, but preferably for a year.
>
> Moving is a big deal, a huge life change and not an endeavor to be taken lightly. It's also exhausting, just as grief is exhausting. Two tiring processes at the same time can be a recipe for disaster.
>
> . . .The decision to move deserves much more thought than a knee-jerk reaction. You may see moving as a way to escape having to face the reminders of your loved one, but it also may not even be a financially wise decision in the long run.
>
> As the months go on, you may find that living in your space is not as bad as you had originally thought. In fact, there may be some comfort in it.[2]

We realized that if we moved, the memory would still be there anyway. We would just be trying to run from it, unsuccessfully, and we'd be leaving behind a multitude of wonderful memories in our home of almost twenty years. We revisited the option of moving after six months and again after a year, and we both continue to feel that moving would hurt our hearts more than help.

I looked up the list that ranks stressful events in life.[3] The most stressful, according to Holmes and Rahe, the first to create such a list, is losing a spouse. Other lists later updated the original with additional events. Loss of a close family member other than the spouse came in at number three. An attempted suicide in the family came in at number four. I found those lists critically lacking. Loss of a child seems to be rolled up with loss of a close family member. Losing my child isn't on the same level as losing even the most beloved aunt. Attempted suicide is listed, but successful suicide is not. As I reflected on these lists with my friend Pat, who lost her husband about seven months before we lost Trevor, she stated that losing a child would have to be at the same level as losing a spouse. I haven't lost my spouse. I haven't experienced the constant intense loneliness of losing my husband of many years, waking without his head on the pillow next to mine, being in an empty house without his familiar footsteps and voice. But I believe, based on my own experience and watching others go through the loss of a spouse and loss of a child, those two traumas are pretty close. A loss such as ours has to come in very closely behind losing a spouse. A spouse is a part of you; you're one flesh. A child is also a part of you. But it's not a contest. When I sit with a friend who has lost a spouse, I don't think either of us is thinking that one loss is greater than the other. We just know that we're both hurting deeply and life will never be the same. We share a bond that others can't understand.

People came and went daily in our home. Our church family embraced us and loved us well, providing companionship, meals, comfort, and much practical help. We cherished every hug. Every hug was someone saying, "Here, let me help you carry that burden." The dryer vent flap broke. With a second-floor laundry room, the outside vent required a long ladder. Steve had replaced that little flap that tended to fall off quite a few times, but this time the job eluded him. He finally conceded that his fog was not going to lift enough to do that familiar chore and called a friend. Dave showed up quickly and the vent was fixed within minutes.

Grief Fog

The trauma cleanup crew finished their job, but the bedroom now needed considerable work. We didn't want to see it; we couldn't see it, not yet. It was too soon. We agreed that we didn't want to see it until all signs of The Event were gone. We put in a call to a friend who had been our go-to handyman for years, knowing that he was a perfectionist in all his work and that we could trust him not to need us to oversee anything he needed to do. John surveyed the job and told us what we needed to choose from the hardware store. He would take care of figuring out other basic materials needed, like drywall and flooring.

If you lost a child to a gunshot, especially if you found him or her, you know the damage we were dealing with. For others, just think "shotgun pellets and lots of damage" and leave it at that. I will not describe the damage any further. No one needs that in their minds.

Steve and I headed to the hardware store. The house we're in now is the fourth house we've owned, and historically we've needed a minimum of a month to select a paint color. We scrutinize all the possible shades of the color we're considering and narrow it down to a dozen or so, take the paint chips home and narrow it down again, then tape them to the wall we intend to paint and look at them in the different lighting through the day for a week or two before finally making the final choice. This day, we entered Lowe's, chose a paint color in fifteen minutes, chose new window blinds five minutes later, and everything else on the list by another fifteen minutes later. As we exited the store, paint chips in hand and photos on my phone of all the other things John needed us to decide on, we saw a mattress store on the other side of the parking lot. We knew our bed was gone. We weren't sure what else had been disposed of. Exhausted from our Lowe's trip, we headed over anyway, just wanting to get the process over with. Fully expecting to have to lie down on a hundred mattresses, we succumbed to the first one we tried. Those salesmen knew what they were doing! They led us to a much more expensive bed than we would ever have chosen if we were thinking clearly. Because of my back issues, I'm very picky about my mattress, so finding one that we would both like seemed an insurmountable undertaking, but there we were, both completely comfortable on the very first one we tried. We had already talked to our insurance company, which had emailed me a form to keep track of what needed replacing. We saved all our receipts and let go of the financial worries. That did not work out as we expected, but I'll get to that in chapter eight. In hindsight, we're relieved to have a completely different kind of bed, a fancy one in a larger size than we've ever owned and with the function of raising the head or foot with the push of a button on a remote. We needed the bedroom to be different, not just repaired. We asked for delivery to be delayed without explaining why, just that we weren't ready for it yet. We gave John our choices and our Lowe's credit card and left it all in his able hands, crumbling into our chairs in the living room, overwhelmed and again overflowing with tears.

Unbeknownst to each other at first, Steve and I both parked ourselves in the Psalms. Dr. Tim Keller says, "There is no better place to wait for God then deep inside the Psalter."[4] I needed to rest in my Lord. I needed to be in the Word and to pray. Sometimes my eyes read the words and, in my fog, I barely comprehended them, yet they ministered to me. As I read, the Psalms were my prayers. "Listen to my words, Lord, consider my lament. Hear my cry for help, my King and my God," (Psalm 5:1,2). "I am bowed down and brought very low; all day long I go about mourning. My back is filled with searing pain; there is no health in my body. I am feeble and utterly crushed; I groan in anguish of heart," (Psalm 38:6–8), about the crushing weight of our sin, but fitting for what I needed to pray. "Praise be to the Lord, for he has heard my cry for mercy." I read, "The Lord is my strength and my shield; my heart trusts in him, and he helps me. My heart leaps for joy" (Psalm 28:6,7) as I pondered how the Lord was providing daily for our many needs. "Let me hear joy and gladness; let the bones you have crushed rejoice" (Psalm 51:8). These and so many other Psalms expressed what I couldn't find words for myself. I read from the Bible app on my phone, my actual Bible being inaccessible in our bedroom. A few days into the week, an Amazon package arrived on the porch addressed to me. Inside was a Psalms journal, an anonymous gift. Amazed and giving thanks, I marveled at how someone had sent exactly what I needed. I puzzled over who had sent it. Several weeks later, the gift-giver identified herself, wanting to make sure I had received it. Dear LaNette! How could she have known I didn't have access to my own Bible?! She didn't. She had sensed God leading her to that particular gift and listened. That journal, at first a place to write down my feelings, the story, and the long journey, eventually became the basis for this book. She also sent me silk roses, with the message, "Flowers shouldn't die. Neither should people." She sent me Steven Curtis Chapman's cd of songs written after the death of his youngest daughter in a tragic accident. I can only listen to that cd in the car, alone, as Chapman sings my grief in a way only someone who has been though it can. And LaNette, a poet, wrote a tender, touching poem for my son. It's tucked permanently

Grief Fog

into the front of my Bible. LaNette has the gift of gifting, and she did it well. May God bless her as she has blessed others!

The first tiny parting of the fog came after about a week as I sat praying and began thinking about my Circle of Sorrow, a group of families I prayed for regularly who had lost children in various ways. I hadn't prayed for that dear group of hurting parents, nor for anything else except for relief from my immediate torment, since The Event. I closed my eyes and forced my mental prayer list to the front of my mind. I don't know how other people keep track of those they want to lift in prayer, but in my mind, I have a graph which has grown with twists and subpoints over the years. I pictured my mental graph and sat and prayed for others. I poured out my heart, pleading with God in detail and by name for friends who have suffered with physical challenges for years, for each person in our small group, for the needs in my Bible study group, for friends with difficult family problems, for widows and widowers I know, and of course for the Circle of Sorrow. I had no idea this would happen, but when I finished, my breathing was easier and my heart felt a little less like a lead weight. My anguish was still there, but I had a small bit of peace and actually felt refreshed. How God ministers to us when we seek to minister to others in prayer!

From the first moments after The Event, I clung to God. I had no doubt that He would carry us through, that He held us in the palm of His hand. But not everybody experiences that. C.S. Lewis, in his book, *A Grief Observed*, recounts his feelings after he lost his wife.

> Meanwhile, where is God? This is one of the most disquieting symptoms. When you are happy, so happy that you have no sense of needing Him, so happy that you are tempted to feel His claims upon you as an interruption, if you remember yourself, and turn to Him with gratitude and praise, you will be—or so it feels—welcomed with open arms. But go to Him when your need is desperate, when all other help is vain, and what do you find? A door slammed in your face, and a sound of bolting and double bolting on the inside. After that, silence. You may as well turn away. The longer you wait, the more emphatic the silence will become. There are no lights in the windows. It might be an empty house. Was it ever inhabited? It seemed so once. And that seeming was as strong as this. What can this mean? Why is He so present a commander in our time of prosperity and so very absent a help in time of trouble?[5]

I did not expect to read those words in a book by this renowned author. When I read his *Chronicles of Narnia* series aloud to my children years ago, I couldn't control my tears when I reached the section where Edmund was redeemed by Aslan. As Lewis illustrated the gospel so strikingly, I was filled with gratitude again at the forgiveness I had found at the cross. My children looked at me with puzzled expressions. I could only pray that one day they would feel the same way. Yet this man, who clearly understood scripture so well, felt alone in his grief, as though God had left him. My heart aches for those who feel that way, but they certainly have good company in C.S. Lewis. As he walked his path of grief, praying and staying in the scriptures, he would eventually find deep solace in God. He said,

> When I lay these questions before God I get no answer. But a rather special sort of 'No Answer.' It is not the locked door. It is more like a silent, certainly not uncompassionate, gaze. As though He shook His head not in refusal but waiving the question. Like, 'Peace, child; you don't understand.[6]

His path was quite different from mine, but we ended at the same place: knowing and trusting our Savior even more deeply.

On Tuesday, I woke up on the sofa in the living room, now my bed, still wearing Saturday's clothes. Of the many people who moved through our home those first four days, not one whispered to me that I needed a shower. I'm sure I smelled thoroughly ripe. As friends gathered around us, they understood, and they hugged us long and often, gently loving us as they tried to find practical ways to help. I felt as though I was in a swimming pool in the middle of a moonless night, up to my nose in water, trying to walk to the edge but not knowing which direction to walk, the thickness of the water making my steps slow and unsteady, my lungs barely able to gulp a breath. Memories crept in endlessly, prompted by the tiniest, seemingly benign reminders, causing tears to cascade anew. Every flow of tears reversed any slight lifting of the fog. I read in Psalm 31:9, "Be merciful to me, Lord, for I am in distress; my eyes grow weak with sorrow, my soul and body with grief." I felt that weakness in my body, my mind, and my spirit. I clung to my "Anchor for the soul, firm and secure" (Hebrews 6:19). C. S. Lewis says,

> For in grief nothing 'stays put.' One keeps on emerging from a phase, but it always recurs. Round and round. Everything repeats. Am I going in circles, or dare I hope I am on a spiral?

Grief Fog

But if a spiral, am I going up or down it?[7]

I wanted off the spiral, but, caught in its coils, I continued through the dizzying loops in my brain, struggling to accomplish daily tasks that couldn't wait. Much landed on the back burner, but decisions and details needed to be dealt with, and my father needed to be cared for. We decided not to tell him what had happened. He was already distressed that he needed my care, and felt like a burden, though I assured him he was not. It was my honor to care for him! But knowing about our loss would have made him want to be put in a nursing home, his greatest fear as he had aged. I would not let that happen. Still, I didn't want to be forced to talk about it, and as his mind slowly drifted towards dementia, I knew I would have to repeat the same things too many times. I put a sign outside his door to remind people not to tell him about Trevor. I fed him his meals and cleaned him up chatting about the weather, the classic movies on his TV, or what his other children were up to with as much perkiness as I could fake. Some days, I couldn't drum up the fakeness and fed him in silence, glad for anything on the TV to distract both of us.

Hayley asked what I needed. I asked her if she could get me some socks and a few pairs of shorts. We didn't have access to our clothing. We had asked the cleanup crew to retrieve some clothing for us, but they had brought out only a pile of Steve's t-shirts. I had no energy to request anything specific from them. We would make do. I discovered a load of laundry still in the dryer which contained underwear for both of us and more of Steve's t-shirts, but other than that, mostly towels. Even as she grieved the loss of her little brother, Hayley selflessly focused on me and tried hard to help ease my pain. I know I thanked her numerous times, but I'm sure my words were inadequate for how grateful I felt. She found practical things to do, small things that made a significant difference, all while she was suffering her own deep pain. Stephen, back in Denver now to save his time off for Trevor's memorial service, which was still up in the air, checked in with us and with Hayley as often as he could.

The police called to ask me which funeral home we would be using. An autopsy was required due to the circumstances, and they needed to know where to send Trevor's body once the medical examiner released him. I looked up funeral homes in our area and narrowed it down to two. Conferring with Steve, I told him that one was very convenient and close, but I preferred the other. I didn't want to use the one I regularly drove past. I didn't want that constant reminder. The one we chose turned out to be a valuable help to us. The young woman who met with us showed compassion and gentle patience as we cried through selecting a casket and made other decisions. She never tried to upsell us, but provided us with practical information which she also emailed to me, especially important since I was entirely unable to retain new details well at that point.

After three weeks, Steve wanted to get back into a regular routine, asking his principal to meet with him to make sure she was in agreement that he was ready. For Steve, his first few weeks were the same as mine in some ways, but very different in others. He has always been a nature lover, relishing his daily walks. During those first weeks, walking in our neighborhood, he stopped to talk to anyone he met. That wasn't unusual for him, a social person who enjoyed meeting new people. What was different was his desperate need to share the gospel. He inserted it into every conversation, even when there wasn't actually an opening for it. He has a history of talking non-stop in high-stress situations. I've seen it a number of times in our decades of marriage, but this time, with such severely drastic conditions, his need to talk, not necessarily about the stress, far exceeded any other time I had witnessed. His continuous talking sometimes focused on The Event and sometimes ran down rabbit trails and ended up in completely unrelated places. During every walk, he watched for people to engage with, sharing long conversations with people he barely knew. He spent more time standing and talking on his neighborhood walks during those first weeks than he spent actually walking, always making sure he shared the gospel at some point. As we talked about that later, we realized that he was trying to see someone come to faith to somehow make losing Trevor count for something. He recognized his coping strategy of persistent talking and realized that it would need to be under control before heading back to the classroom. Once he felt able, his principal met with him and agreed that he was ready to return to school. She graciously made sure that he had a light load that first week back, removing some of his normal duties from his plate. For him, getting back to a normal work routine helped to dissipate the fog. For me, left alone to care for my father as he continued to languish in hospice care, my fog settled in as an uninvited long-term guest in my head.

Chapter 3

ACCEPTING HELP

"A friend loves at all times, and a brother is born for adversity" (Proverbs 17:17). Friends knew well before we knew, ourselves, that we needed help. Some things we needed help with were obvious, and others were not. We swallowed our pride and asked. We'd rather be the helpers than the help-ees! Our front door remained open daily from early morning until after dusk with a note covering up the doorbell letting people know that if we knew they were coming, to just come in. If we didn't know, they could knock and then come on in, calling out a "hello" to alert us. We have a silly doorbell song which I couldn't bear to hear right then, and asking people to let themselves in spared us from hearing it and also saved us a small amount of our negligible energy by not requiring us to actually answer the door.

Our church set up a meal schedule, and many hands provided an abundance of healthy food. Under different circumstances, I would have requested recipes, but I would always associate those recipes with The Event and would never make them. Under different circumstances, we would have felt like royalty, with a wide variety of delicious and nourishing meals available with no effort on our parts. We wanted different circumstances! I had no appetite at all, but I sat down and ate breakfast, lunch, and dinner because I knew I needed to. Sometimes as I ate, I thought about how my chef-son would have loved this or that way of preparing a particular food. We received Brussels Sprouts several times, which I had never liked, but, apparently, I had never learned to make them properly. Other people knew how to make them well, and I grew to appreciate them in a new way. They also made me cry, though, as I remembered Trevor preparing them for us. His Brussels Sprouts were delectable! I could have eaten a full dinner plate of them for my entire meal. Many people provided not only suppers for us, but added in snack foods and breakfasts. They knew how deeply we were hurting. They wanted to aid in whatever way they could, trying to help us as we navigated this unfamiliar pain. Providing practically for us enabled them to be a part of encircling us, making sure we knew they walked with us as much as they were able, that we weren't alone. Oh, how thankful I was! I wept when people arrived with food because of the awful reason for our need, but also out of gratitude because they were loving us so well. They stopped and talked with us, which we needed more than the food they brought. What a strange mix of emotions I had, both intense grief and profound thankfulness at the same time. I dreaded having to shop. I had no energy, and couldn't imagine walking through a store making decisions about what to buy. I couldn't imagine finding a parking space to get into the store. Actually, I couldn't imagine even picking up my keys and getting into my car. Never underestimate the value of a meal for a hurting friend.

It was close to a month before I finally needed to shop. As I walked through the store, seeing people casually chatting and laughing together, my mind swirled. How could everyone be so normal? Didn't they know that the whole world had turned into chaos and confusion? Of course, they didn't know, and I fully knew it was unreasonable for me to think they could, but that was how I felt. I paid for my items and rolled toward the exit with my cart, tears at the surface, my breaths choking in my throat, and my heart in a vise grip. As I neared the receipt checker at the door, I saw a female employee instead of either of the two men who regularly attended that spot. I walked past, then suddenly pulled my cart back and sobbed to her, "Can I have a hug?" She answered, "of course!" and wrapped me in her arms. She quietly spoke right into my ear, saying she didn't know what was going on, but that God had me in His hands and then prayed for me. I needed that hug so desperately right then. In the many times I've been in that store since, I've never again seen a woman at that spot, only two older men. It's embarrassing to admit that I asked a total stranger for a hug in a store, but God provided exactly what I needed, and I'm thankful.

Lush green plants and exquisite flower arrangements arrived, bringing a fragrance and beauty that lifted our hearts, albeit momentarily. Before long, our kitchen table had so many plants and flower vases that when friends came to sit with us, we needed to shift the arrangements to be able

Accepting Help

to see each other. It would have made sense to relocate some of them, but we wanted to see them all together, a visible representation of the support of others. When the table became too full to hold anymore, I chose some to put near my temporary bed on the living room sofa. Steve chose a few to put on the deck, where he often sat to read scripture. We'd given plants and flowers to others in the past, but this was the first time we had been recipients of such a large array of beautiful greenery ourselves. As the number of arrangements grew, a verdant garden on the table, they became a constant reminder of God providing tangible support under the crushing weight of grief. And that led us to worship. The individual efforts of many, gathered together in front of us, nursed our souls more than we could have anticipated.

Cards and notes began arriving, and we quickly established a routine of leaving them on the kitchen table between our two dinner seats. We read them aloud together each evening before we ate, both the preprinted words and the personal, written messages. We treasured the words, the love, and the thought nestled in every single card. Someone took the time and effort to select each card, to write in it, address it, put a stamp on it, and get it into the mail. That alone ministered to us more than they may ever know, but the written messages were like a salve gently applied to our wounded hearts. One friend who had also lost a son by his own hand, one who had been childhood friends with our boys, sent a card in which she said, "It's okay to laugh." I needed to hear that. I needed to be reminded that we had to continue on with life. All those cards are saved, tucked into a special container to be brought back out at the right times, perhaps on anniversaries of The Event or on Trevor's birthday. Several people took note of Trevor's birthday and sent cards when that date came around. I saw one of those women in church the day after we received her birthday-remembrance card. I fell into her open arms and wept into her hair, "Thank you for remembering my son!" Sending a card to a hurting person may seem like a small thing. I can say unequivocally, every single note and card is significant. Every single one!

Luke 10 tells of a man who was robbed, beaten, and left for dead. We weren't physically beaten, and we weren't robbed, though we felt as though both had happened. A Samaritan came across that man and, without regard for himself, stepped in to care for him. He nursed the beaten man's wounds and provided for a safe place to recover. The family of Christ became the Good Samaritan to us, attending to needs that were beyond our capabilities at that point. Our garage door opener stopped working. It wasn't the first time. I had fixed it a number of times before. But in trying to reprogram it, I broke a switch. A deacon from church was on it. John finished the work in our bedroom, but he doesn't do carpeting. Again, the same dear deacon, who owns a construction company, got his people on it so we wouldn't have to see the room with the repaired flooring still showing. We had no idea of the expenses that were about to engulf us. Other people knew. Friends, family, and our church immediately gifted us with financial help. As God often does, He blessed us with what we needed immediately, but not beyond. Agur, son of Jakeh said in Proverbs 30:7–9,

> Two things I ask of you, Lord;
> do not refuse me before I die:
> Keep falsehood and lies far from me;
> give me neither poverty nor riches,
> but give me only my daily bread.
> Otherwise, I may have too much and disown you
> and say, 'Who is the Lord?'
> Or I may become poor and steal,
> and so dishonor the name of my God.

Everything that had to be paid immediately was able to be paid off. Expenses that could be delayed went onto credit cards or a payment plan. Today, we're still chipping away at the remaining costs, but it's manageable, and we're not overwhelmed. The generosity of those who so quickly pitched in, who loved us so deeply, still stuns us. To be clear, in response to the Proverb quoted above, it's highly unlikely we would have been tempted to steal, but there was no need because of God's gracious provision. His people heard His call and answered, as we're urged in Hebrews 13:16, "And do not forget to do good and to share with others, for with such sacrifices God is pleased." I feel as though I overuse the word grateful, but every use is completely appropriate. I lack a better word, other than to add an adverb. I could say truthfully that I'm immensely, extremely, utterly, abundantly, mightily, and tremendously grateful.

Many people told us that if we needed anything at all, we could call them. I always expressed deep, heartfelt thanks, and usually ten minutes later my brain struggled to remember who had offered. Brain fog would kick in for the hundredth time, or two hundredth. If you have someone in your life who is engulfed in grief, please send them something in writing, a text or an email, because they will probably forget who offered what.

Accepting Help

Many did just that. We received regular texts and emails reminding us that people were praying and asking if we had any particular needs. Once Steve went back to work, my greatest need emotionally was to see my precious grandchildren. My father, though, couldn't be left alone. I put out an offer to pay people to come sit in our house for a few hours, not to be actual caregivers, but just to be present in case of an emergency. A number of people responded to that request, all of them refusing any kind of payment. One in particular, John, a different one from our handyman, not only regularly came and sat with my dad, but texted me every week to make sure I had someone. He has a quiet history of ministering to many others in similar ways. We should all be doing that! I hope he knows how much his presence blessed me, not only because I was able to see the grandkids, but because that act of consistently reaching out to me before I reached out to him ministered to my throbbing heart.

Our two grandchildren, a balm to our souls every time we see them, couldn't come to our house. They were aware that Uncle Trevor had died, but they weren't told how it happened. Hayley wisely told them simply that he had a sickness in his brain that made him die. But since our bedroom, a main play area for them, was blocked off with plastic hung over the doorway and over the carpeting in front of it, they would have wanted to know what was going on and begged to see it. We wouldn't lie to them, but we obviously couldn't explain the truth to them, nor let them see the damaged room. When the time eventually came for them to return, we told them that we had repainted our bedroom and gotten a new bed. They didn't need to know why, and being children, it didn't occur to them to ask. The entire room had changed, but they accepted that we had just freshened it up and questioned nothing. At some point when they're older, they will hear the fuller story, when their parents feel they're ready. That won't be my decision to make, but I don't fret about it. I know my daughter and son-in-law will be on top of it. The child who is biological needs to be aware that it's in her genes and that some form of mental illness could possibly strike her when she reaches her teens and twenties. Being alert to the possibility may help her to accept and deal with it in a healthy way, should it affect her. We have many family members who have never been affected by mental illness, but a few who have, and knowing that there is a history makes it seem prudent to have a conversation with her at the right time. The adopted grandchild needs to hear the same things, because we just don't know which kids may be affected and which won't, and we don't know the medical history of his biological family. Most of all, they need to know there is no shame in having mental illness and that there are treatments available. I've gained a much deeper compassion for those with mental illness, having seen it up close and personal. No one chooses mental illness. Some do make life choices that make it worse, but no one makes a decision for their brains to not work as expected.

Quite a few people gave us books. How grateful we were to have printed words of comfort, advice, and wisdom from people who knew grief themselves! I've always been an avid reader, but for the past two years, I haven't read anything other than books on grief or suffering. I'm sure I'll eventually get back to reading for the pure enjoyment of it, but for now, light reading seems vacuous to me. That's just me, of course. For others, literature other than grief books can be the vital escape that we so desperately need as we navigate the murky waters of grief. I find better escape in old familiar movies or a sitcom or two, which others would probably find a waste of time. Steve has never enjoyed sitcoms. His respite lies in listening to solid sermons which focus him on the Lord. Tim Keller is his go-to almost every evening as he winds down before bed. Each of us needs to figure out for ourselves how best to achieve a temporary reprieve so we can brace ourselves for diving back into the grueling and fatiguing work of grief. And it is work. That work demands us to sit in our emotions, to let ourselves feel them, to sort through them and dig deeply into them, to cry with God and cry out to Him, to search our hearts for whether our guilty feelings are justified, to come to terms with our helplessness, to forgive and receive forgiveness, to figure out if there's any way to actually ever make sense of all that happened, and so much more. Yes, it's work, and it's hard work. We learned that sometimes we needed to stop trying to work so hard. There's no road map for this journey. We usually didn't know the next direction to even venture a step towards. We sank into the familiar scripture from Psalm 46, to be still and know that He is God, but in a new and more profound way, letting go of our questions and longings and sitting with our God, acknowledging our sadness and confusion but releasing our desire to get on to the next stage, past this intense pain. The work still needed doing, but grievers need to know when to stop working and press pause, nestled in the palm of God's hand.

We retreated from the news. Steve, usually a news junkie, wanted to read or hear nothing about current events. I was less addicted, but routinely watched the first twenty minutes of both the main stream media news and the conservative news channels, comparing the coverage and trying to find unbiased middle ground. Now I didn't care. I tried to watch the TV shows I had enjoyed in the past, but artificial scenes of murder and death shook me, and I deleted those shows. The true crime documentary type shows that used to fascinate me as I watched how detectives unraveled a crime made me think of the distressed mothers of the victims in the stories. I cried for those moms, and I deleted those shows, too. I would watch only old, safe, movies.

I also turned to my computer for help. I could no longer remember the name of the gang Trevor had mentioned. That horrible grief fog destroyed so many details, but I understand that the fog of grief protects us from being completely swallowed up. I did remember the first letter of the gang. I searched for names of gangs in Richmond and found a site with lists for every city in Virginia. There was no gang listed in Richmond or in any other city that started with that letter. Did I remember incorrectly what he told me? Had he intentionally told me the wrong name of the gang, thinking he was protecting me? I had to wonder if there had truly been any gang threats at all towards Trevor. In his paranoia, had he imagined this gang? As we continued to learn more by talking to his friends and reading about paranoia, I realized that was a clear possibility, or more likely, a probability.

When life is "normal" and stable, most people juggle the daily ups and downs with varying degrees of finesse, rolling with the occasional inconveniences. We no longer had any kind of normal, and we didn't know if or when we ever would again. Daily ups and downs constantly pushed our heads under the deep waters, making us gasp for air as we sought to resolve issues that wouldn't have even been issues in the past, like getting our cars in for inspection on time, or just remembering to sit down and pay the bills. As we struggled to deal with those things, another problem cropped up. Trevor's car wasn't anywhere to be found. Steve and Hayley separately walked and drove for blocks around both his apartment and his work, searching unsuccessfully. I gave Hayley his license plate number and keys, and she put out a call on one of her social media platforms asking local friends to be on the lookout for it. I texted Anna-Mae and asked if she had any idea where he might have parked it. She didn't. The next day, someone contacted Hayley. They had found the car! A few hours later, Anna-Mae also texted that she had spotted it and sent me the same location Hayley had been given. Relieved, Hayley and her husband headed out to retrieve it, but it wouldn't start. We wondered if Trevor had parked there purposely, trying to keep his car from being easily spotted by people who were looking for him, and then the car just wouldn't start again, or if he had broken down and somehow managed to get it over to the curb. With the extreme paranoia he had been exhibiting and with the condition of the car, either case was plausible. Considering the neat parking job, we leaned towards thinking he had wanted to hide it from the people he believed were after him. After Hayley and her husband attempted to jump it without success, we called our car insurance road service, the same company Trevor had his own policy with. Steve talked to the tow truck driver, explaining that we weren't the owners but we were now responsible for the car and why. The driver kindly agreed not only to tow it to our mechanic friend's house close to an hour away, but to do it for free, considering the circumstances. How amazing to see yet another way God provided, so unlike what we expected from the road service, which typically provided towing only within a certain number of miles. Our friend, a car-mechanic-turned-firefighter, looked at it and felt it wasn't worth fixing unless it held sentimental value to us. Although he was happy to help us if that was what we wanted, he suggested it might be better used by donating it to the fire department for training purposes. We thought Trevor would have liked that, and we signed the title over to them. They would dispose of it properly once it was beyond use for training. One more task behind us, we marveled at the circle of people who enabled the car to be found, towed, assessed, and repurposed. Our weary hearts could let go of one more task.

After a week of sleeping on our sofa, I yearned to fall asleep to music rather than old movies. Old movies distracted me enough so I could fall asleep without my mind replaying The Event over and over and over again, but I sensed I needed to fill my mind with worship instead. My earbuds were in the bedroom, and thus inaccessible. The penny-pincher in me moaned, even though my earbuds were cheap ones, but practicality won out, and I ordered another pair. They came in a day, and I quickly began looking forward to immersing myself in worship music as I drifted off to the blessed relief of sleep. I chose artists whose lyrics were particularly worshipful to me. I needed to be lost in pure worship, in the truths of who God is, to be marveling at His grace, His love, His goodness, His power, and His holiness. What a difference that sweet worship made for my sleep! I focused on the lyrics, my heart relaxing, my mind pondering the truths I knew, and I had peace. I was almost always asleep before the chosen album ended. The one frustrating part of using earbuds was that they thought I wanted them to turn off, rewind, or skip a song if one touched my pillow. I quickly started using one only in the upward-facing ear, but even then, if I reached to adjust it, it sometimes turned off. Our neighbors, who are believers and friends, learned of how I was falling asleep, and also why I used only one earbud. Joe and Sandy appeared at my front door with earbuds meant for sleeping. Touching them wouldn't advance or rewind music or turn it off. Again, I was so blessed in such a practical and meaningful way by people who prayed for us and thought through our needs. My heart cried with thankfulness.

In his job as a public-school teacher, Steve can't openly share his faith, but he's free to have conversations with people who initiate them. The year before, a student had been going through a tough time and, sensing that he was a Christian, asked to talk to him. Her faith came out, which enabled him to talk to her about the Lord and help her to apply some scriptures to her life. When Steve started back to school three weeks into the new school year, that student ran into him and said, "Hi, Mr. Wozny! I don't know why, but God told me to pray for you over the summer!" Steve was dumbfounded, and as a result, she was one of the few students to whom Steve revealed that he had lost his son. She and her aunt, who had experienced some deep losses of her own, sent us each a gift bag with items specially chosen to comfort us, including a cd of various worship songs. They had clearly culled their choices carefully and intentionally. I put that cd into my phone as a playlist, and it became a regular part of my nighttime worship. I'm sure this dear student and her aunt prayed that the songs they chose would be just the right ones. God answered those prayers as He profoundly brought me to worship through those songs. I still listen to that playlist at night regularly. Psalm 147:1 says, "Praise the Lord. How good it is to sing praises to our God, how pleasant and fitting to praise Him!" As I listened to accomplished musicians playing and singing to the Lord, my heart was able to rejoice and to sing with them. Falling asleep was often the best time of the day, not only because I needed sleep, but because I fell asleep worshipping the God who knew my pain and who held me in His hand.

"Carry each other's burdens, and in this way you will fulfill the law of Christ," we're told in Galatians 6:2. Dave, the retired Colonel and army ranger Steve had told Trevor could get him to safety, along with his wife, my dear friend Ann came often to sit with us, pray with us, and share scriptures with us. Ann texted with me regularly asking if I had needs she could help with, as well as sending me lyrics to meaningful hymns and links to helpful messages. She somehow knew exactly how to balance her texts so that she ministered to me consistently yet didn't overwhelm me. Dave was able to get Steve out of the house, taking him on a long bike ride on Richmond's Capitol Trail. Being outside in nature with a close buddy next to him to talk to helped Steve to progress in processing his grief. Dave and Ann, both great listeners, blessed us tremendously in those first weeks, offering wise insights gleaned from what we shared but without trying to "fix" us.

Friends and family not only helped us carry our burden with practical help, they also jumped in to take over commitments we couldn't fulfill. Our small group at church circled around us, not only providing meals, companionship, and prayer, but also lifting responsibilities off our shoulders. Our co-leaders for the group stepped up to shoulder all the leadership responsibilities for the entire next year. Much as we love our group, leadership takes energy and clear thinking, neither of which we had. Bob and Valerie loved us well in taking the sole leadership roles for an extended period of time. It cost them in time and energy, but they made it clear that they fully expected us to step away until we felt able to come back into leadership, however long it took. We gratefully accepted a sabbatical from leading, and the entire group continued to minister to us lovingly, praying with and for us, as well as weeping with us. They gave us a beautiful wood and metal windchime engraved with the words, "When someone you love becomes a memory, the memory becomes a treasure." They didn't know when they chose that windchime that Treasure was one of Trevor's childhood nicknames. I decided to hang it inside in a spot where I can, when I want to, deliberately circle through the downstairs in the opposite direction from normal just so I can brush against the windchime and think both about Trevor and about the love shown to us by our small group.

I have a spot at church where I get to serve each week running the PowerPoint from the sound booth. It's a little niche for me, a spot I've been allowed to dominate because my back issues prevent me from serving in so many other areas. Many years ago, someone at church provided me with a chair better suited for my pain issues than the regular chairs in the sanctuary. When the church expanded, the music director made sure the chairs he purchased for the new sound booth would continue to meet my pain needs. I have my chair and heating pad and am a happy camper in my little spot on Sunday mornings. As the A/V needs of the church grew and changed, I grew with them and never trained anyone else for the position. I had a few people I had asked years ago to be emergency fill-ins and had written up emergency instructions just in case, but a fill-in was never needed. Unfortunately, it had been so long since I had prepared those contingency plans that all but one of the people on the list had moved away. Zac, the remaining person from that list, had since become ordained and taken on considerably more responsibility in serving the church. But he jumped on the need before I even remembered. I got a text from him a few hours after he left our home that first day, letting me know that my spot was covered for the next morning and that I could let go of even thinking about it for the foreseeable future. A staff member, Jen, accepted the request to be my sub and quickly learned the behind-the-scenes routine. I discovered only much later that the emergency plans I had written up were dismally out of date since equipment had been updated and systems changed. Jen figured it all out and ran everything as though she had done it for years. I gratefully let go of thinking about my little spot of ministry. We should all be serving in some way at our churches, but none of us is indispensable. I was the only one entrenched in the PowerPoint part of ministry on Sunday mornings, but God provided an able person to immediately take over with graciousness and skill. As an elder, Steve was currently on the break from session that our church requires every few years so the elders don't burn out. His other functions as an elder, such as serving communion, were taken over by other elders, much to his relief. We love our church, and we're grateful that they've blessed us with places to serve. We're equally grateful that others could take our places for a time.

Many people reached out to simply sit and listen and pray with us. As people gathered around our kitchen table, weeping with us and seeking to somehow soothe our anguish, we talked. Sometimes we talked too much. No one ever asked us to share less. I'm certain that some people heard more than they really wanted to hear. Later, I would feel the need to pray that God would protect their hearts from the hard details that some of them heard. Yet talking, we realized in hindsight, helped us to process the entire scenario and to slowly emerge from the fog. It was vital. As the days crept by, each still smothering us in a murky mist, we gradually began to comprehend that the path set out before us through this dark tunnel, revealing no light whatsoever at the end, would be an unending journey. One day, we might see some light in the distance. We might even step to the end of the tunnel and gaze out at streaming sunshine, but one foot would forever remain firmly in that tunnel. Our lives were forever changed. A few friends who had lost children themselves especially understood that the journey has no end. They embraced us firmly: physically, mentally, emotionally, and spiritually. They helped prepare us for that realization by listening and sharing from their own experiences. Butch and Judy encouraged us with "It doesn't get easy. But it gets lighter." Judy told us that over time they had moved from thinking "why" to instead asking God what should be next, how He might use them through the tragedy they had experienced. This is a club that nobody wants to be a member of. But members we are, members in the dreadful club of parents who have lost children.

We kept our word to Anna-Mae, asking her to our home for dinner several times. I also met her for coffee down near Trevor's old apartment. In our home, Anna-Mae shared stories with us of the last few years as she and Trevor had dated. She filled in gaps and told us a few things that no parent really wants to hear, but which we very much needed to know. Anna-Mae struggles with mental illness herself and has done much research. We quickly saw how brilliant she is, a deep thinker but with many issues she continues to struggle with. She described to us how Trevor used LSD. She would take 1–3 "tabs," she said, but he would take 7–10 at a time. He didn't do drugs often, but when he did, he took a lot. He took more at a time than anyone else she had ever seen. As we grappled with that, we realized that one of the results of his self-medicating was that he had most likely damaged his already-fragile brain even more. Oh, how this hurt to hear! Anna-Mae told us stories and we told her many, too. I mentioned that his favorite color was red. She looked at me with a puzzled expression and said, "No, it was green." I thought about that, and I came to the conclusion that my little boy, who had loved red up through his teen years, had grown up and perhaps had changed. He doted on his plants, which lent credibility to his change of favorite color, but what most convinced me was his graffiti handle, LOP, which was almost always in green. But as I write this, his phone lies on my desk next to me in a red case. What Trevor's actual favorite color was will now always be a question mark to me, and as insignificant as it may seem, it saddens my heart. These things matter to a mother who has lost her child.

Anna-Mae walked with me all over the area where she and Trevor had lived, showing me places they had loved to hang out, as well as spotting his stickers, which apparently are a "thing" for young artists. They design and order stickers, then leave them on sign posts, public scooters, telephone poles, and other places to show off their artwork. As the weeks passed, Anna-Mae wrestled enormously with her grief, needing to be hospitalized several times. From her own experience as well as her research, she felt that

Accepting Help

Trevor had been suffering from paranoid schizophrenia. We'll never know for sure, but it does fit what we saw during his last three days. Anna-Mae eventually moved an hour or so away back near her family to get a fresh start. Richmond held too many difficult memories for her. She took Bill, the smelly cat, with her, much to our relief. She loved Bill as though he was her child and was thrilled when we happily relinquished him to her. We would keep Trevor's other rescue cat, Phasma. When Trevor's permanent headstone finally arrived and was installed, over a year and a half after The Event, I texted with Anna-Mae to let her know. I also wanted to tell her that I had found two tiny marble kittens and a swatch of Trevor-like fabric when I was cleaning up the temporary marker I had placed on his lonely plot, sad that only sparse wispy grass graced it. As soon as I saw those kittens, I knew they were from her. I brought them home so they wouldn't be discarded by workers who would soon be preparing the spot for the permanent marker, then took them back and placed them carefully, mostly hidden, so Anna-Mae would know where they were if she visited Trevor there again.

Several months after The Event, I heard the tragic news that a woman in one of our sister churches had lost her husband. He had gone out for a run, leaving his wife and toddler at home as usual. He stepped in the back door upon his return, had a heart attack, and passed away before his wife even knew he was in the house. In less than a week, there were signups for an entire year for meals, house-cleaning, and child-care. I felt a pang of jealousy that lasted for about 20 seconds or so. We needed help desperately as we walked through our family tragedy, but as I pondered the amount of help that other woman was receiving, I felt that it was too much. She had months off of work, her house was clean, her cooking was done, and her child was being cared for by others. I lamented for her that her friends were inadvertently prolonging her grief. Part of moving through grief involves getting back to some sort of normalcy, whatever that may look like in light of our losses. I quickly moved from wishing people would clean my house for a year to being grateful that I had received just enough help, not too much or too little. In his booklet, *Grieving a Suicide: Help for the Aftershock*, Dr. David Powlison says,

> You might have little interest in your work or household responsibilities, but you need to keep going. Take time to grieve, to process. . .and get back to normal living. Doing these things makes a statement that life continues despite what has happened.[8]

God tells us to pray, "Give us today our daily bread," (Matthew 6:24). We can focus on our needs today, just today, as we wade through the river that grief is. We don't need to worry about the entire next month, much less year, regardless of any help we are or aren't receiving. Even in our grief, we can have peace and don't need to be consumed by our upcoming needs. We can pray for today's needs, then be still and know that He is God (Psalm 46:10). As we consciously put this into practice, we found we were able to let our attention shift to intentionally focusing on our grief. This grief required work. It wasn't going to simply fade away. We needed to grapple with it, wrestling the painful questions that accompany such a loss.

Steve was able to connect with a grief counselor early on. His counselor helped him wade through the raging waters, working through his feelings of helplessness, guilt, and just plain missing his son. With my dad still in our home in hospice care, I couldn't leave for counseling. The precious times people could come to relieve me were reserved for grandchild time. I did what many before me had already done. I found and joined a private online support group only for parents who had lost a child to suicide. The administrators of the group vetted each person who asked to join to make sure we were all sharing the same type of loss. It was startling to see how many were in the group. There were thousands! For every post someone wrote, the responders numbered anywhere from a dozen to hundreds. I read through post after post, understanding exactly what the poster meant, tears streaming down my face. Sometimes I asked questions, other times I was able to respond to someone else's post in a helpful and supportive way, and often I just read, learned, and grieved. My father passed away in November of that year, outliving his grandson by three months. I began official grief counseling shortly thereafter. My counselor, whom I'll call Ruth, worked within a Christian organization, and her bio stated that she counseled from a Christian perspective. For the first session, she mostly just listened to what had happened. If she was going to help me, she needed to understand how it had all unfolded and hear enough details of the day to assess me appropriately. I used half a box of tissues in retelling the horrible story. She suggested that I bring in photos of Trevor the next time. When I did, she smiled and, "Oh, you brought pictures! What a wonderful idea!" I was startled. She seemed not to remember that she had asked me to bring them. She asked me what my goals were for our sessions. That question threw me off. I was there for grief counseling. My goal was to get through my grief in as healthy a way as possible. I thought the grief counselor would know that. I answered that I hoped she could help me sort out all the chaotic emotions of grief. She used an analogy of a river to describe grief, how sometimes the water was flowing gently and sometimes it was rough. I liked that image and added that I was on a raft in the river, a raft that held me carefully and would never throw me off, that my raft was Christ, bringing me through the rapids safely. Ruth responded enthusiastically, "Oh yes, and sometimes you might get off the raft and climb around on the rocks." Get off my raft? Leave Jesus? She hadn't understood my reference to Christ at all. I found that distressing. Still, that evening as Steve and I talked, he too liked the river analogy. After that, instead of asking each other how our grief was that day, a question that elicited pain just in the asking, we began asking how our river was. That one little word change helped us. The following week, during my third session, Ruth assessed me for PTSD. Because I had entered the room and witnessed the details of the scene up close, she was concerned. She decided that she didn't feel I had PTSD, but told me that if I started having nightmares or a lot of flashbacks, we would need to revisit it. I do see the scene again in my mind regularly, but I haven't had nightmares, so I'm remaining in a wait-and-see mindset. She told me that the next week we would discuss the stages of grief. That day came, and for that fourth session, there was no mention of the stages of grief. I suspected that she either didn't take good notes or didn't review her notes before a new session. I was troubled that this Christian counselor had yet to share a single scripture with me and had never once prayed with me. I mentioned to her that at church, I could no longer sing. I love to sing to the Lord with others, and I missed it, but I broke into tears whenever I tried to open my mouth. I asked her if she had any thoughts on why that might be happening. She looked at me blankly and said, "the Holy Spirit?" I know that much of counseling involves just listening and rephrasing, but that's pretty much all she did. At this session, she finally attempted to offer a scripture. She couldn't remember it, she said, but it had to do with 'Because of what God has done in me, now God's people can surround me and help me.' She asked if that sounded familiar and I had to say it didn't. I thought perhaps it was a muddled version of 2 Corinthians 1:3–4, "Praise be to the God and Father of our Lord Jesus Christ, the Father of compassion and the God of all comfort, who comforts us in all our troubles, so that we can comfort those in any trouble with the comfort we ourselves receive from God." When I mentioned how much seeing my grandchildren helped me, Ruth smiled and said enthusiastically, "Oh, I sure understand that!" I naturally responded by asking her how many grandchildren she had. She had none. I asked her how many children she had. She had none. I discreetly looked at her ring finger, which was unadorned. Somehow, her enthusiasm over the blessing of grandchildren now seemed disingenuous. The only helpful nugget I received from her in four sessions was the river analogy. With her lack of scripture in counseling and her seeming to forget what we had talked about from week to week, I decided to end our counseling relationship. I then disregarded the advice I've given others in the past: If a counselor isn't a good fit, it's not written in stone. Don't give up, just move on to someone else until you find the right one for you. Instead, I returned to my online group, the ones who fully understood and gathered around me every time I needed them. With a number of Christians in the group, I felt cocooned with sound understanding and helpful words. We all, Christians and non-Christians alike, were in the same situation. We understood what no one else did. We knew how it felt for our children to take their own lives.

Most of the people who surrounded us with help in so many ways really didn't understand, nor did we expect or want them to. A few people said, "I can't even imagine." Don't. Please, don't. I really didn't want them to imagine this horror. They couldn't, and it wouldn't help them in any way. If God ever asked them to step into a similar journey, then alone would be the time for them to feel this torment. What we did want and need was what countless people gave: help. Help came in the form of caring words and hugs, of silently being with us, of prayers, of practical acts of service, of notes and texts, of scriptures at just the right times, of financial and other gifts, all given selflessly and with genuine love and concern. I don't even know all the people who helped us. We kept track from the beginning of those we did know of, wanting to make sure we sent each one a personal thanks. I designed a special thank you card, one that I'll never use again for any other purpose. I made a list in my computer of whom I had written to, correctly guessing that I would forget. I referred to that list many times as I wrote eighty-three thank you notes, which didn't include thanks for the many cards we received. I wanted to thank those people, too, but Steve wisely suggested, as he watched me write a note, then take a break to ice my wrist, that I needed to abandon the desire to not leave anyone out. My heart both ached and swelled with gratefulness at the love so many poured out for us. Over the next two years, as people slowly moved back from surrounding us quite so tightly, God regularly brought people to me to say, "I still keep Trevor's guitar pick in my wallet to remind me to pray for you," or

Accepting Help

"I listened to this song and it reminded me of you; here's a link to it," or to just give me a meaningful hug. Our family, church family, and friends have loved us well. Our God has loved us well.

> God is our refuge and strength,
> an ever-present help in trouble.
> Therefore we will not fear, though the earth give way
> and the mountains fall into the heart of the sea,
> though its waters roar and foam
> and the mountains quake with their surging. (Psalm 46:1–3)

Chapter 4

GUILT, STIGMA, AND THE UNFORGIVABLE SIN

Even before I became a believer at the age of twenty-one, and having no prior teaching about Christianity, I had heard mention of the Unforgivable Sin. As I grew as a Christian in a solid, Biblical church, I learned that although all of our sin separates us from God, the one and only sin that can't be forgiven is denying that Jesus paid the penalty for all those other sins. When we understand the incredible sacrifice that Christ made by dying, paying the penalty for sin, that is, death, and when we believe that and profess it, we are utterly and completely forgiven for every sin, past, present and future. 1 John 1:9 says, "If we confess our sins, he is faithful and just and will forgive us our sins and purify us from all unrighteousness." In Ephesians 1:7 we read, "In him we have redemption through his blood, the forgiveness of sins, in accordance with the riches of God's grace" and further down in verses 13 and 14, "And you also were included in Christ when you heard the message of truth, the gospel of your salvation. When you believed, you were marked in him with a seal, the promised Holy Spirit, who is a deposit guaranteeing our inheritance until the redemption of those who are God's possession—to the praise of his glory." In Romans 8:38, 39 Paul assures us "For I am convinced that neither death nor life, neither angels nor demons, neither the present nor the future, nor any powers, neither height nor depth, nor anything else in all creation, will be able to separate us from the love of God that is in Christ Jesus our Lord." If our sins are as far from the Lord as the east is from the west (Psalm 103) once we've placed our faith in the shed blood of Jesus, then we can release the misconception that suicide is unforgivable. It's a sin, of course, the sin of self-murder. Can murder be forgiven? Yes, as with any other sin, bar one. The only sin that can't be forgiven is to refuse the forgiveness offered to us. In an interview by Czarina Ong on September 18, 2015, Kay Warren, wife of pastor and author Rick Warren (*The Purpose Driven Life*), whose son took his life in 2013 at the age of 27, says,

> God promised us that Matthew's salvation was safe and secure. Matthew gave his life to Jesus when he was a little boy. And so, I'm absolutely 100 percent confident based on the work of Jesus that Matthew is in Heaven. And that's a certain hope.[9]

Steve and I witnessed Trevor's prayers over his last three days, his tearful pouring out of his distress, as well as his praises to the God he loved, and we are certain that he was genuine and is now in Heaven. But there are many Christians who have lost a child to suicide who simply don't know where their child was spiritually. I pondered and searched this. I think most people would agree that those with mental illness, though not "mentally disabled" in the traditional sense, are not able to think clearly. We certainly saw that in Trevor on his last day. They lack entirely the capability to process information as others do. Insights for Living says,

> As Christians, we know that Christ's death paid for all sins and that God extends forgiveness to all who believe in His Son. But what about infants and mentally disabled individuals who *cannot* believe in Jesus? God's merciful and compassionate character suggests that grace is applied to them as well (Matthew 18:14; Romans 5:18–19). In fact, Jesus called the children to Himself, actively taking a role in their well-being (Matthew 19:14).
>
> With these factors in mind, we can affirm that an infant's or mentally disabled person's inability to articulate faith in Jesus does not prevent God from saving him or her. And God, in His compassion and mercy, would draw these individuals to Himself in heaven based on the sacrifice of Christ for all sins.[10]

Of course, that's not the final word on the subject. We don't know. We can't know. We search the scriptures and read what wise people have learned by doing the same, and then we have no choice but to rest in what we understand about God. That's not a bad thing! He has a particular grace for those who can't fully understand His truths. We do know that. We expect that some will judge Trevor on their own and determine that he couldn't possibly be in Heaven, but that contradicts scripture. We have no doubt that

Trevor is healthy and whole with his Savior, worshipping at His feet with no more pain or suffering.

Yet suicide brings with it a judgment by others not only on the victim, but on the survivors, the victim's family. The fog of grief prevented us in the beginning from feeling the shame of our child having taken his own life, but the guilt was immediate. Thoughts of the many ways we had failed Trevor consumed us, and we talked through tears for hours about what else we could have and should have done. Had we ruined his life? Could we have gotten help for him, even against his will? We dug back in our memories to his earliest days, remembering his happiness, his sunny smile, and his silliness, trying to pinpoint when it all changed. We remembered when one of his many nicknames was Smiley Boy, because his face constantly shined with his sweet, bright smile. Our conversation traveled through all the stages of his life. Normal activities like T-ball, learning to ride a bike, creating with Legos, family game nights, developing a love for reading, and voluntarily helping me in my gardens filled his early childhood. As we looked back, we saw no signs of unhappiness until we moved to Virginia's Eastern Shore, where we all experienced loneliness and regret at having left a community we loved. Steve and I now pored over that decision, dissecting it repeatedly, and each time came to the same conclusion. We had done what we needed to do. We had bathed it in prayer and done our best to make a wise decision. If we had to do it again, without the benefit of hindsight we would make the same decision. As soon as Steve could start a new job search without seeming to be a job-hopper, he had put out resumés and we got out of Dodge. We got settled in Richmond and I committed to transporting the kids to any and all activities they had the slightest interest in. I wanted desperately for them to find their niches. With vastly different personalities, each of them experienced their own unique issues as they figured out how to fit in. Steve and I pondered how we could have made that transition easier and better for them. We came up empty. We're flawed. We did the best we could. We had gotten them involved with youth group, we got the boys involved with other homeschoolers to play in a softball league and to learn Spanish together, and we spent lots of time with each other as a family, hiking, playing games, playing music, and just being together. As with any parents, every day presented some circumstance or other where we could have handled things better. Our kids apologized to us many times for being disrespectful or not doing something they were supposed to do. We also apologized to them for too many times when we spoke too quickly before understanding a situation correctly, for over-reacting to small things, and for sometimes just being flat out wrong. But our kids knew we loved them unconditionally. We were a normal family. As Steve and I searched our broken hearts trying to work through our guilt, we eventually concluded that even though we had made mistakes galore in raising our kids, they had happy childhoods and we had done the best we were capable of. In a post on August 11, 2021, the Survivors of Suicide Loss website says to all, like us, who need to hear these words,

> People die by suicide not because of what you have or have not done for them, they die because of their pain. It was not the words we said or did not say. They die by suicide and take with them many of the answers we seek. Without those answers, it is much easier to point the finger at yourself. It is much easier to blame yourself. . . . Unfortunately, this is what many suicide loss survivors do.[11]

The article goes on to discuss how we don't want to blame the victim for his or her own suicide, and with the impossibility of ever getting the answers we lack, we place ourselves as the villains in the heartbreaking tragedy, convincing ourselves that we somehow had the power to prevent it from happening. The reality of others blaming us hit me hard when, several months after The Event, I received a phone call from the police. The officer informed me that Trevor's case was officially closed. Officially closed? I didn't know there was a case open. That phone call staggered my heart as I thought about an officer reading the autopsy report and listening to the recording of the 911 call to decide whether we had a hand in our son's leaving. I hadn't known the police were assessing whether I was guilty. I cried again, deeply, as I recalled all the details of that wretched day, hard enough on its own, but compounded with the recognition that others were determining in their own minds whether we were guilty in some way for Trevor's action.

But there is a difference between guilt and responsibility. While you may feel guilt, most likely false guilt, over not having done something differently, that doesn't make you responsible for that person's action. Stacey Freedenthal, PhD, LCSW, states,

> The tricky thing about self-blame is that, even though it hurts intensely, it also protects us from a greater pain. In blaming ourselves, we nurture the illusion that we have some control over life. . . .When someone dies by suicide, it is never one person's fault. Not yours, not someone else's, and not the suicide victim's.

> Instead, the fault belongs to *the natural forces that create the potential for suicide*. Most often, these forces are mental illness. By many accounts, 90% of people who die by suicide have a diagnosable mental illness.[12]

Dr. Freedenthal suggests wise questions to ask ourselves as we flounder in feelings of guilt. The weight of guilt as we try to grieve often prevents us from thinking clearly about how much control we had or could have had over our child's suicide. As parents, we want to think our influence over our child, no matter their age, supersedes their ability to act on their own. We know that's not true, yet we keep yanking that lie back into our brains and the guilt festers. Consider these questions Dr. Freedenthal poses:

> Am I telling myself that I could have prevented my loved one's suicide?
>
> How do I know that, even if I had done things differently, my loved one would still be alive?
>
> How could I have known then what I know now?
>
> Can I feel compassion for myself for having said or done things that I desperately wish I could change?
>
> Can I forgive myself for being imperfect?[13]

Even as I work though these questions, there are days when I have to recite to myself on repeat, "It was not my fault, it was not my fault, it was not my fault." We know as Christians there is an invisible, infernal enemy. Satan would like nothing better than to have us sink in our grief, overcome by feelings of guilt, and to become useless in the Kingdom of God, or even to deny God altogether. Once we've worked through those debilitating feelings of guilt, we need to let go of them and stop taking them back. We forgive others, as we state when we say The Lord's Prayer (Matthew 6:9–13) and hopefully in our private times of repentance before the Lord. We need to accept God's forgiveness, and then also forgive ourselves. James 4:7 says, "Submit yourselves, then, to God. Resist the devil, and he will flee from you." We need to continually turn to the scriptures, ponder the truths we know about our Lord, and pray, focusing on worship first and foremost.

As the reality of Trevor's action set in, we slowly recognized the shame that accompanied it for us, and along with it, the stigma. We agreed early on that we would not hide Trevor's cause of death, though we didn't include it in his obituary. Suicide needs to be talked about. It's not talked about because the family is embarrassed for having failed their child and because they want to protect his reputation. We hate that Trevor will always be remembered as a young man who took his own life.

Even more, we realized that when others learned how our child's life ended, judgment was inevitable. After the publicity surrounding a celebrity's suicide a number of years ago, I remember thinking what a selfish way to die suicide is. The victim leaves behind others to work through their sorrow and pain with no answers, to wonder about what they did wrong, and to clean up that person's lose ends. Often, there was no goodbye, no apology for the pain caused, and no opportunity to even attempt to help. After watching Trevor slowly unravel over the three days he spent with us before escaping his pain, I will never again think suicide was anyone's selfish way out. I witnessed that Trevor had suffered from mental illness and that he had been in a deep, dark hole, one so deep that he couldn't see out of it. He won so many of his battles with mental illness, but he lost the war. I don't believe his suicide was a choice, and thus there was no selfishness in it. To be a choice insinuates that he was able to rationally think through his options and come to a conclusion. Watching him spiral down, we saw that his paranoia utterly blinded him. He was completely devoid of the ability to contemplate the pros and cons of anything, especially something of such staggering enormity. Steve and I agreed that we would be open about how Trevor had died and work through the pain that admitting it would bring. We anticipated that people would be kind to us, but some, perhaps many, would be thinking about what kind of horrible parents we must have been that our child had to take his life to get away from his pain. I went through GriefShare[14] classes, an international program which helps people who are going through grief from many different types of losses. A young couple from a different church who took that class with me had lost their child to cancer. I mentioned as I talked with the wife that it's been difficult to work through the additional levels that accompany loss due to suicide. She was puzzled and asked what I meant. I told her that when a child is lost by his own hand, there's a judgement from others, as well as a deep guilt that we should have been able to see it coming and done something to prevent it. She disagreed that I had a level to my grief that she didn't have. She told me that she felt guilt, too, and that people were probably judging her as well. I just nodded. I wasn't going to continue that conversation with another grieving mom. It's not a contest. But when the video hosts of GriefShare, David and Nancy Guthrie, mentioned that suicide carries with it unique aspects of grief, I saw that woman turn her head and gaze at me for just a second. I felt sadly validated in my feelings when the Guthries recognized that suicide leaves the survivors with aspects of grief to work through that others don't have. The other woman hugged me after the session. No words were needed. She understood, but so many never do. That's the stigma that parents of suicide victims face, that we're permanently labeled bad parents and all-around dreadful people. As Christians, the stigma and shame were magnified, not by our church family, but by non-believers who misunderstand what Christianity is. We know that we're sinners and that nothing in us can make us acceptable to God on our own. We know that the only way to come before God is by having an intermediary, someone who could pay the price we can't pay on our own to erase our sinfulness, the sin that plagues us daily, even though we try so hard to curb it. But people unfamiliar with the Bible commonly think we believe that we're better than they are, that we think we've somehow gained the power in ourselves to become pleasing to God. Some of those people, we realized, were thinking that we had gotten our just desserts for thinking we were better. Nobody said it out loud. It's something we could see in their eyes. Pastor Kurt Ebert, in talking about changes in himself a number of years after his sixteen-year-old son took his life, said,

> [I was] maybe a little less judgmental. I would have to say before this ever happened to me if I heard of somebody taking their life in a family, somebody's kid, there was always this thought; I don't think I would ever say it out loud, but I think I would have thought to myself, 'I wonder what they did wrong.' And now I know the answer: nothing! They were being parents. They were doing the very best they could, and something happened.[15]

We can't stop others from thinking and feeling as they do, but we can leave the door to conversation open. If this sickening nightmare should ever happen to one of them, perhaps they'll come to us. Perhaps God will allow us to use our own horrifying tragedy to help them. How do we deal with the shame and stigma? We pray. We praise. We reflect on how God carries us through each day, how His mercies are new every morning. We repent for our pride, for letting what others think bother us. We don't deny how painful every aspect of our grief is, but we turn to God, over and over, and find our rest there. We thank Him for those who have wept with us, and we pray that one day we also will "weep with those who weep" (Romans 12:15 ESV). We ask God to use this agonizing and degrading journey to somehow glorify Himself and to allow it to help someone else in the future.

Recently I was reading in the book of Luke and came to the passage where the angel told Mary she would conceive and bear a son. She listened, a girl of probably fourteen or fifteen, and no doubt knew immediately that she would face scorn and shame, yet she responded, "May it be to me as You have said," (Luke 1:38). Can we say the same as God allows this unwanted journey in our lives? Can we trust that He who knows the number of hairs on our heads, who knows the sparrow that falls, who clothes the lilies of the field with all their glory, is holding us in the palm of His hand, His very able and powerful hand, and that He loves us more than we can comprehend? I had an epiphany at some point during those first days. Trevor, deep in a hole he couldn't rescue himself from, was rescued by God. Our boy, our beautiful boy, came to us in his distress, and then he came back to the Lord. As I pondered all that had happened, it occurred to me that God had taken our boy while he was walking closely with Him, before he had a chance to return to the things that had pulled him farther and farther from God. I researched the treatments available for paranoid schizophrenia. If Trevor had somehow been able to survive his unraveling, he was facing a lifetime of trying to pinpoint the medications that would help his particular brain and would need regular therapy indefinitely. Trevor hadn't even been willing to get treatment for his intense foot pain! For years he had resisted every plea from us and others to seek help for his depression. The likelihood of his following through with treatments to help his mental illness would have been negligible. What a merciful God we have, that He allowed this tragedy, as horrible as it was, and relieved Trevor's inevitable suffering for the rest of his life and that He allowed us to see our child return to faith before The Event happened. What a contradictory set of emotions I have, deep grief mixed with deep gratitude. Lord, may it be to me as You have said.

Chapter 5

MEMORIAL SERVICE

We waited a month before having a service to remember our beautiful boy. With workers coming and going daily to repair our bedroom, with the pile of belongings to deal with, and with my father being in hospice care at our house, we agreed that an immediate service was too much for us to handle. As the shock slowly dissipated, though, we needed to make some decisions. Our church gently asked questions about what we wanted and helped us nail down a date. Lynn, our church administrator, asked me if we wanted a reception afterwards. Dear Lynn heard a dazed "I don't know" from me numerous times. I said "I guess so," and she told me not to give it another thought, to consider it done. Many of us have planned weddings, enjoying months of pouring attention into every minute detail, pondering myriads of choices, and with much excited anticipation. Planning a funeral, though, especially under the circumstances we were enduring, is quite a different thing. The relief that I could completely let go of thinking about a reception actually brought me to tears.

Zac would deliver the eulogy. He sat with us, talking about Trevor and hearing stories of his childhood. We told him that we didn't want to hide that he had taken his own life. It needs to be talked about. The suicide rate for young people has skyrocketed in recent years, and maybe our being open about Trevor's death would help some other family. Maybe they would recognize our story in their own child. Maybe conversations would happen that wouldn't have otherwise. According to the CDC, suicide is the second leading cause of death for people in Trevor's age range. Deaths due to suicide in the US are almost double the deaths due to homicide.[16] We talked about songs that we would especially like to include and scriptures that we'd like read and who we would like to do those readings. We struggled with what to call Trevor's funeral service. We felt that calling it a "Celebration of Life" was somehow disingenuous. His last ten years had been filled with pain and depression. The torment of his final years hardly seemed like something to celebrate. We settled on Service of Remembrance. We would remember the happier times and also recognize his suffering. Then we relinquished control of the service into Zac's trusted hands. We could concentrate on the tasks we needed to complete and let go of the rest. Uncharacteristically for me, letting go of control turned out to be both effortless and a relief. Our church lived out Galatians 6:10 to us, "Therefore, as we have opportunity, let us do good to all people, especially to those who belong to the family of believers."

In the week following The Event, Steve wrote a lullaby for Trevor. It came to his mind complete, both music and lyrics, and he wanted to play it during the service. Our kids and I urged him not to, anticipating that he would break down in tears and not be able to finish it. He wisely listened. He called the church's music director, Michael, who came to our house with Joe, one of our many accomplished musicians. They listened to the song, recorded it on a cell phone, and left fifteen minutes later assuring Steve that they would present his lullaby exactly as he wanted.

I've made memorial videos for quite a few people in the past, setting photos to music especially chosen by the family. I have more weaknesses than I want to admit, things I simply can't do well or at all, but I've been able to create some striking memorial videos, an art that I accidently fell into. I knew early on how I wanted Trevor's to be, and I knew that I needed to do it myself. I pulled out old photo albums and scanned favorite pictures, and Anna-Mae provided more recent photos to fill in the scant folder of his last couple of years. In 2011, Trevor performed at our church talent show, flawlessly playing a rendition of Stevie Ray Vaughn's *Lenny*. In the video of that performance, one person can be heard through the thunderous applause at the end shouting, "Daaa-amn!" Now there's something I had never heard in church before! Joe, a skilled musician himself, the same Joe who was now working on Steve's lullaby for Trevor, came up to me after that performance with wide eyes and said, "Your boy can play!" I used the video of that performance as the background of his memorial video, occasionally dropping away the photos to show him playing the music they were set to. I cried steadily as I worked. How could I be making a memorial video for my own child? Steve chose not to see the video until the service, and I worked with headphones so he wouldn't hear our beautiful boy playing, with snippets of lines played repeatedly as I carefully edited the length of the display time for each individual photo so it would flow with the music but not be on a distinct rhythm. I elaborated with text on some, such as the group photo of the *Adventure Boys*, the photo where he stood on a bench in downtown Philadelphia with an arm outstretched pretending to be a statue to coax a pigeon to land on him, and the photo of painting his bedroom orange. He thought we would nix orange, but I told him that when he grew up and got married, his wife would never allow it, so this was the time to have an orange bedroom. Thinking about his never having that wife to tell him he couldn't paint their bedroom orange crushed me. But the video turned out better than I had hoped for, and I breathed a sigh of relief as I closed Final Cut and sent the finished product to a flash drive.

With the date set, we worked on practical details. We needed someone to be with my father so we could all be at the service. My sister was willing, but she also wanted to be at the service to support us. Her willingness to be wherever we needed her drenched my heart with gratefulness. The hospice program allowed for a certain number of hours of a caregiver sitting with the patient so the family could be away. They were sorely understaffed, though, and it looked unlikely that they could provide some help for the date we needed. Our hospice nurses came to the rescue, intervening for us and explaining our excruciating circumstances. The program pushed us to the top of the list and found a woman to help us. My sister would attend the service and pop into the reception for a while, then relieve the hospice worker so we could spend the rest of the day with old friends who were traveling from Pennsylvania to support us.

Steve's best man from our wedding and his wife notified us that they would be coming from Connecticut for the service. Scott and Bonnie have been dear to us since before we married. Steve, Scott, and I spent time together before we got engaged, resulting in Scott giving Steve his whole-hearted approval of me. We sang in Scott and Bonnie's wedding when we were engaged, and they participated in ours a year later. When Scott called to tell us they were coming to the service, Steve instantly asked them to stay with us. My adrenaline rushed at the overwhelming thought of my ultra-introverted self, in deep grief, needing to entertain friends, even those as dear as Scott and Bonnie. I would need to provide meals and be a gracious hostess. I couldn't do it. I begged Steve to ask Butch and Judy to put them up, knowing they would do it in a heartbeat, but he was adamant that they should stay with us. They would be arriving by bus on Friday afternoon and staying until Monday or Tuesday. Steve assured me that it would be fine and that it was the right thing to do. My feathers remained ruffled and I persevered in requesting every now and then that he rethink it. He insisted that he wanted Scott, a close companion since his early days as a believer, to be in our home so they could have extra time together. He needed Scott. I knew he was right. I finally acquiesced and resigned myself to conjuring up my elusive hospitable side. I was exhausted just thinking about it. I asked Steve to at least be home from school before they arrived, to which he promptly agreed, understanding my tension. The day for their arrival came, and Steve was not home when I heard a tapping on the front door. There they were, their kind, familiar faces, creased with concern as they gazed worriedly at me through the storm door. We hugged and I escorted them to the kitchen, where we all settled in and started talking. God knew what I needed so much better than I did! Scott and Bonnie were medicine to my soul! We talked comfortably about their trip, and I told them some of the details about The Event and about the service planned for the next day. I felt completely at ease and encompassed by love. They graciously slept on the pullout sofa in Steve's study, comfortable for one, not so much for two, while we continued with our makeshift beds in the living room, on the couch and on the floor in a sleeping bag. When we woke up in the morning, Steve and I showered and dressed, but Scott and Bonnie remained upstairs. Shortly before it was time to go, they appeared, completely ready and having breakfasted on granola bars they had brought with them. They had wanted to give us privacy as we prepared our hearts for the unimaginable, the funeral of one of our children. As we drove to the church, Scott read Psalms to us and prayed, and again I felt encompassed by support and love. How could I have not wanted them to stay with us? They brought us exactly what we needed. God knew!

At the church, we were escorted to a private room to await the start of the service. Having run A/V for other memorial services, I knew that the family would be sequestered, but I had never experienced it myself. The room looked quite different from this new perspective. I didn't like the new look. We nervously picked at food and chatted uncomfortably as we contemplated this public recognition of the horrible tragedy engulfing us. The other grandparents drove to Richmond to care for our five-year-old grandson, who was too young and antsy to sit through a service, but our eight-year-old granddaughter attended. When we were led to the sanctuary, she lovingly clung to my side and chose the seat next to me. How odd the sanctuary appeared. The back of the church was solidly packed, but the front was just sprinkled with attenders. Is this what happens when the death being recognized is a suicide? Were people uncomfortable and mentally wanting to keep some distance from the agony of the loss? Had the first people to arrive chosen the back and everyone else just followed suit? It was a little unsettling, but I could ponder that later. I focused on controlling my breathing and not crying.

Michael had taken charge of all things musical. The team he recruited included people who had known Trevor and people who were especially significant to us. He couldn't have assembled a more meaningful group. Every time we stood for a song, my granddaughter, with whom I have a special bond, stood next to me, squeezing my hand. As an unchurched child, she wasn't familiar with the songs, but her comforting hand in mine communicated that her heart was sharing in the song, even if her voice didn't. We came to *Amazing Grace*, a hymn Trevor had mentioned was especially meaningful to him. As I sang, thinking of my boy now at the feet of Jesus Himself, once lost but now found, I suddenly heard a clear, sweet voice rising up from my granddaughter. She knew *Amazing Grace*! Although her family didn't go to a church, she attended a private Episcopal school and had heard it there. I sank back to my seat and put my arm around her as we shared the precious words of the hymn together, grateful for the gift of this child by my side. For me, that was one of the most meaningful moments of the entire service, our love and our sadness mingled together in song, a child of the past gone, while this child representing the future nestled next to me.

Steve, Hayley, Stephen, and I had debated on who should speak at the service. All three of them said they wanted to say something, so I felt I should, too. Steve said he wanted to share last, and I opted to go first so I wouldn't be sweating waiting for my turn. Hayley and Stephen were amenable to being in the middle. One of my strongest weaknesses is getting up in front of people to speak, but when I need to, I will bathe it in prayer and trust that God will be my ever-present help. I began writing out a list of special memories of my sweet boy to share with a sea of both familiar and unfamiliar faces. I finally admitted to myself that I'd never make it through all the memories I wanted to impart and settled on just one. I told about the best gift I've ever gotten, other than Jesus. When Trevor was about four years old, he came out of his room one morning and gave me his normal sunshiny smile, and I told him he could wish me a happy birthday today. He gasped, hugged me, and then ran back into his room, closing the door behind him. A few minutes later, he emerged with a bandanna-wrapped bundle in his hands. He handed it to me, beaming, and told me "Happy birthday!" I carefully unfolded the bandanna to find a framed photo of his beloved teddy bear, Nosey. He was our teddy bear boy, having dozens, each with a carefully-selected name. But Nosey was his first and favorite, his constant companion, and the photo he gave me had sat where he could see it from his bed. My heart melted, and I asked him, "Oh, Honey, are you sure you want to give this to me? You love this picture!" He grinned at me and said, "That's what makes it a good gift!" That was my Trevor's heart, and that photo has been on a wall or a shelf in my bedroom in every home we've had since. I got through the memory I wanted to share, my voice cracking, and was glad I had kept it short. Hayley and Stephen both shared what they wanted to say about their brother, and then Steve's turn came. He was still in a state of non-stop talking, and we all worried about how he would handle his time at the podium. He assured us that he was in control. He shared some special memories of Trevor, poignantly and eloquently. He shared how Trevor had come back to the Lord and illuminated the gospel, knowing that there were many in attendance who didn't know what scripture says about our sin and our need for a Savior. But he couldn't turn off. His sharing time slowly transformed into a sermon. I stood nearby on the stage, wondering how to reign him in. Zac would be delivering a eulogy. This was a sharing time, a time to remember our son, to paint a picture of his personality and gifts. After what seemed like a few decades had passed, I walked over to him and put my arm around him, gently tapping him on his back. He immediately recognized that he had gotten lost in speech and brought it to a close. A dear friend had agreed to videotape the service for us. We couldn't watch it for a long time, but as I worked on this book, I wanted to go back, to hear what had been said when I was still lost in fog. As I listened to Steve share on the video, every word was cogent and appropriate. He went down some rabbit trails, as he is prone to do, and he went way over his promised three minutes, speaking for over eighteen minutes, but what he shared was earnest, heartfelt, and captivating. He honored Trevor, and he honored God. When Steve arrived home on the day I finally watched the video, I told him, and his eyes teared up as he asked me if what he had shared was completely out in left field. Someone had told him he was mentally unstable in the weeks following Trevor's death, and he agonized that he had embarrassed himself and dishonored Trevor's memory on the stage at the memorial service. Now I firmly avowed that he had not, that what he had shared was entirely coherent and fitting. I fetched my computer and set it before him, queueing up the sharing time. We wept as we watched together. As it ended, he turned to me sobbing with both renewed grief and with relief, saying, "I wasn't off the rails! I wasn't!" I wished we had watched the video sooner. We could clearly see that he wasn't mentally unstable. He was simply a father in deep grief who coped by talking.

As the service continued, Steve's lullaby for Trevor stilled the entire room. Michael, along with Joe, his brother Brad, and Chris, had blossomed Steve's guitar notes and lyrics into a gentle, calming, waft of beauty. Michael's voice cracked with tears on the last line. Steve would never have made it through.

Lulla Bye by Steve Wozny

Sleep child
Rest your head
We'll be leaving soon
Dream about
The day ahead
The birds, the trees, the moon
It's late
We've got some things to do
While you're asleep, it's true
It's only just a little bit
For we are sleepy too
The day we planned's
Been changed
But only re-arranged
A better plan
By One who can
Make better plans come true
So rest your head
My dreamy boy
We'll all be leaving soon
And when you wake
We'll be right there
We'll be right there with you

Memorial Service

The receiving line at the reception stretched farther than I could see from where I stood. Steve, still in talking mode, had a conversation with every person in line. I admire that he was able to do that. I wanted to lie down alone in a dark closet to cry, but the hugs I received ministered to me more than any closet floor would have. Friends helping with the reception whispered in my ear numerous times, asking if I needed a chair. Yes, I did, but I refused it, knowing I would later regret missing even a single hug due to sitting down. My granddaughter worried that I wasn't getting to eat and occasionally appeared at my side to tug my hand and say, "Come on, Grammy, you need to eat!" Touched at her sensitivity, I gave her suggestions every time she returned, foods that she could set aside for me next to her own chair. For over an hour, we greeted, hugged and were prayed for by loving friends and family from near and far. Eventually, I collapsed next to my granddaughter and she delightedly pointed out all the food choices she had gathered for me. One day I hope she'll understand how much her presence that day meant to me. Slowly, people trickled out. Friends who had traveled far to be there followed us back to our house for additional time together. We talked until dusk, when they needed to get going, while my sister took care of our dad's needs. Scott and Bonnie remained, a deep solace to our weary minds, bodies, and souls.

Hayley and Stephen requested that only the immediate family attend the burial on Monday morning, and we agreed. Scott and Bonnie tended to my father. When we arrived, the casket was already in place. Chairs lined one side, and the four of us sat. The gray casket encased our boy, hiding him from one last view of his treasured face. We had each given something to the funeral home to be placed into the casket with him. I put in his paints and paint brushes. During the Covid pandemic, he had taken up drawing and painting. He had talent, and I especially loved the sketches he had done with hands in various positions, notoriously hard to draw. I couldn't bring myself to mingle his paints with my own. It seemed fitting to put them with him. Steve added a memento from his walk with Trevor the previous July, when he had first reconnected with us. What Hayley and Stephen put in are not for me to write about, being part of their own stories to share if and when they choose. As we sat there, I knew that Trevor wasn't really *there*. It was only his body. But I was overcome with knowing that his body *was* right there, only feet away but unreachable, and I suddenly stood up and placed both hands on the casket, desperately wanting nothing more than one last hug. My body heaved with sobs, my tears washing over the gray metal, unable to reach my boy. We asked if we were allowed to put in the first dirt once the casket was lowered. "Of course," we were told, and a small shovel was provided. Steve and I ignored the shovel and knelt in the fresh dirt, our four hands gently dropping a cascade of soil into the hole. He was in a hole again, but not the deep hole of mental illness. From that, he was finally forever free.

> Very truly I tell you, whoever hears my word and believes him who sent me has eternal life and will not be judged but has crossed over from death to life. (John 5:24)
>
> Though he brings grief, he will show compassion, so great is his unfailing love. (Lamentations 5:32)

Chapter 6

THE PHYSICAL TOLL

How many tears poured from my eyes? Looking back, I don't think I'm exaggerating to say that I cried more tears in the first few months after losing Trevor than I had in my entire life before that. Scripture says poetically that God collects our tears in a bottle (Psalm 56, ESV). He must have an incredibly large bottle to hold all my tears! My distress was so deep that from the first moment it happened, I didn't care who saw me cry, or how hard, or when, or where. Sometime in those first weeks, I learned that tears of grief are different from tears due to an irritation, like cutting onions or a speck of dirt in the eye. One article from The Cleveland Clinic helped me to understand

> [emotional] tears gush in response to strong emotions like sadness, grief, joy or rage. They have the same chemical makeup as basal tears [the normal continual moisture in our eyes], but contain more stress hormones and natural painkillers.[17]

Tears of grief are actually cathartic. I determined that I would not try to hold back tears. If they needed to come, they could come and were welcome to stay for as long as necessary. My tears were a gift from God to help relieve the profound pain, even if only momentarily.

The grief fog held its grip for several months. It slowly waned, to both my relief and my dismay. I longed for the protection of that fog as I waded forward with an aching heart. One day I began having chest pain. I have a minor heart issue that occasionally causes pain but requires no treatment. I chalked it up to that and ignored it. Several days later, though, the pain was continuing and intensifying, not the normal fleeting pain I was familiar with. It was increasingly hard to ignore. Alarmed, I started paying attention. I recall lying on my bed resting one afternoon, intentionally focusing on the pain and trying to discern how it was different and wondering if ignoring it was wise. It increased in regularity and lasted for minutes to hours. Heart pain is not something to shrug off, but in typical Keallie-fashion, rather than head to the ER, I headed to my computer. The pain wasn't radiating down my arm or up into my jaw, as a heart attack often does. Considering our circumstances, I suspected it was related to grief. I searched for symptoms of a broken heart. I found that a loss such as ours can indeed cause symptoms like I was experiencing. Cornerstone Hospice says,

> Some grieving people literally become 'heartsore.' You may begin to experience chest tightness, pressure in the throat and chest, or chest pain. These symptoms result from your body's reaction to stress, which can result from any stage of the grieving process.[18]

Many sites that impressed me as reputable, such as The American Heart Association, discussed Broken Heart Syndrome. I learned it's more likely to happen to women than men and is often misdiagnosed as a heart attack. It's caused when "a part of your heart temporarily enlarges and doesn't pump well, while the rest of your heart functions normally or with even more forceful contractions."[19]

I considered whether or not I needed to see a doctor and whether I needed to tell my husband. Steve, already dealing with deep heartache, didn't need another layer of worry. I knew him well enough to anticipate he would panic, thinking he was about to lose his wife on top of losing his son. I decided not to tell him about this heart pain.

I had already seen my general practitioner, but that was before these symptoms began. As I read, it seemed that many people experience heart pain after losing a loved one, which relieved my anxiety substantially. This was "normal," I realized. It wasn't good, but it was normal. My understanding was that if it continued, it could become serious, a condition called Broken Heart Syndrome. Medication is generally used with Broken Heart Syndrome, and it tends to be effective. But I didn't feel I was at that point. I'm not a doctor, and I wouldn't advise anyone else in my situation to simply watch and wait, but that's what I chose to do. Should I have gotten checked out just to be sure? Probably, and that's what I would advise others to do. Because learning about what was most likely going on gave me such relief, I was comfortable with waiting. If the pain had worsened, I would have acted, but it slowly retreated, and within a few weeks, it had dissipated. I never knew there was actually such a thing as a broken heart. Steve's last words to Trevor were, "You'll break your mother's heart!" How true those words turned out to be.

Backing up a bit to that visit with my general practitioner, I had already had that appointment on the calendar scheduled for about a month after Trevor left us. I dragged myself to his office, and when Dr. Port entered the room with his usual congenial greeting, my "Hello" was already choking in my throat. I knew I needed to tell him. He took one look at me, sat down and leaned towards me, asking with deep concern, "What's going on?" I tried to get the words out. My breaths heaved as I gathered the courage to utter the loss out loud, finally blurting out, "I lost my youngest son." The tears started pouring. I knew I needed to say more, that I needed help and that Dr. Port needed to know. "He took his own life," I choked out. "In our home, in our bedroom." Shock and compassion on his face, he talked with me. Whatever patients anticipated him in adjoining rooms would wait. He had long prescribed a medication to help me sleep with my back issues, and now he urged me to take it more often. Although it's non-addictive, I didn't want to rely on a prescription to sleep, using it only for higher pain times. But these were new circumstances, and I agreed to use it as he suggested. He suggested grief counseling and also offered to increase the anti-depressant I was already on for chronic pain. He lived up to the reputation he already had in my mind, an outstanding, compassionate, and medically competent physician who listened well. At that point, I began alternating my over-the-counter sleep aid with the prescription, finding each more effective by flip-flopping them. Sleep can be frightening for those going through grief. Sometimes it simply eludes us as we lie awake thinking about our loss in the quiet darkness. But for some, sleep is interrupted by nightmares, reliving the horrible tragedy and trying to force a different ending. For me, using a sleep aid every night plus using earbuds to listen to worship music until I fell asleep helped me to avoid lying awake with my thoughts going to hard places. I did use the higher dose of the anti-depressant, but it made me even more numb. I felt that I needed to go through the pain of grief in order to progress and that the anti-depressant, while making me a little less sad, was making me feel anesthetized and stationary. There's no way through grief except through it, and I felt like the increased numbness from the antidepressant was hindering my grief rather than helping. I tapered it back to my usual dosage, with my doctor's approval.

Each day in the beginning, my only goals were to brush my teeth and eat something. I vaguely saw movement in the bathroom mirror in front of me, but I was merely going through the motions, just getting the bare necessities accomplished in a haze. I would trudge into the bathroom in the morning and try to remember what I was supposed to do. 'Oh, brush my teeth. Wait, there's something else that's part of the morning routine. Oh, wash my face.' I stumbled through each day trying to make old habits normal again. One day, a month or so into this journey, I actually looked into the mirror for the first time. What I saw startled me. Returning my gaze was a woman ten years older, pale and sad. My eyes contained no spark, my hair was drab, and I looked thinner than usual. I've always been extremely thin with a tiny bone structure, making me look a bit gaunt. I had long ago come to terms with being overly skinny. I am "fearfully and wonderfully made," says Psalm 139, and God made me exceptionally thin. But this new skinnier me looked unhealthy, almost skeletal. I stepped on the scales and saw that I had lost seven pounds. For me, that was a lot. I began paying better attention to my food intake, making sure I ate three meals of healthy food and at least one high-calorie snack during the day. A month later, I had lost another three pounds. It's probably more common to gain weight after a tremendous loss, but for some, it's the opposite. Many people would love to have this problem, but it's not delightful. A full year later, I had managed to gain only four pounds by eating ice cream daily. Admittedly, there is some delight in a good bowl of mint chocolate chip, but the excessively slow progress in getting back to my normal weight frustrated and concerned me. Then I was hit with a pneumonia serious enough to be hospitalized, and my hard-won four pounds disappeared. Once home, I experienced complications that made my recovery last for months rather than weeks. Puzzled at my difficulty in healing, I searched online for answers. I found in an article on WebMD that

> Grief increases inflammation, which can worsen health problems you already have and cause new ones. It batters the immune system, leaving you depleted and vulnerable to infection.[20]

In the past, I was rarely sick, catching only an occasional cold. Now, for two Christmases in a row, I had lain in bed, so sick I could barely acknowledge the holiday. During the second one, when I was hospitalized with pneumonia, I was also nursing a broken toe. As I recovered from pneumonia, the toe stubbornly refused to heal. When I was finally able to see an orthopedist almost three months after I brutalized that poor toe on the edge of a wooden stand, I learned that the anti-inflammatories I had been taking morning and night for the prolonged complications of my pneumonia had interfered with bone growth and prevented healing. In addition, I discovered, again at my trusty keyboard, that in a study on bone healing, researchers had found that

> ...psychological trauma and other massively stressful experiences slow down the healing of bone fractures... The research team, which included scientists from Canada and Japan, was able to demonstrate that certain immune cells respond to stress by producing an enzyme, which in turn promotes the release of stress hormones. These stress hormones act locally on the bone where they inhibit the conversion of cartilage cells into bone cells, thus slowing down bone growth and fracture healing.[21]

Not only my use of anti-inflammatories, but also my grief itself was apparently keeping that tiny bone from healing. The amazingly created complicated systems in our bodies interact to keep everything healthy and running smoothly, but they also interact to disrupt the health we so often take for granted. In an article about grief and gut health, Nuala Mcbride discusses how our bodies may react to the deep stress of grief by not absorbing nutrition normally. She says,

> Grief can have a notable impact on gut health. The connection between the brain and the gut, known as the gut-brain axis, means that emotional distress can manifest physically in the digestive system. The stress associated with grief may disrupt the balance of the gut microbiota, leading to changes in digestion and absorption of nutrients.[22]

In hindsight, it seems that my body was failing to process nutrition well even though I was eating healthy foods, and I slowly declined into a vulnerable condition at risk for illness. In the hospital, bloodwork showed that some of my levels were off, one of which indicated possible anemia. Follow up bloodwork a week after I was discharged showed that I was leaning towards anemia. Anemia can depress the immune system, which is already depressed in a person going through grief. Was my shift towards anemia enough to push my immune system even lower? Possibly. Whether it was or not, though, it was no wonder that my body was experiencing continued health issues. The gray-looking face peering at me from the mirror reflected the outward manifestations of the distressful internal physical changes in my body due to grief.

Although I was eating well, I had stopped exercising, other than playing with my grandchildren. With a broken toe and pneumonia complications, including shortness of breath with very little exertion, walking was difficult, but I knew I needed to at least try. As my lungs regained their health, I buddy-wrapped my toe and hit the treadmill, walking carefully, but walking, walking, walking. I added in some arm strengthening on a weight machine, suspecting that at least some of my weight loss was due to muscle loss. My weak, skinny arms looked more pathetic than they ever had. I was as consistent as I was able in being as active as my body allowed, and by the time the second anniversary arrived, I had gained back seven pounds. When I looked into the mirror in the mornings, I saw a healthier me and sometimes even a smile.

I leaned on my God every day, reading through the Psalms over and over, praying, and remembering God's promises. Over and over in scripture, He tells us He'll never leave us or forsake us, and many passages address God healing us from afflictions of many kinds. Psalm 103:2–5 says,

> Praise the Lord, my soul,
> and forget not all his benefits—
> who forgives all your sins
> and heals all your diseases,
> who redeems your life from the pit
> and crowns you with love and compassion,
> who satisfies your desires with good things
> so that your youth is renewed like the eagle's.

James 5:14–16 tells us,

> Is anyone among you sick? Let them call the elders of the church to pray over them and anoint them with oil in the name of the Lord. And the prayer offered in faith will make the sick person well; the Lord will raise them up. If they have sinned, they will be forgiven. Therefore confess your sins to each other and pray for each other so that you may be healed. The prayer of a righteous person is powerful and effective.

And yet, we also read of God allowing us to suffer physically for His own wise reasons. Paul suffered from some sort of affliction which he referred to as a thorn in his flesh. We read in 2 Corinthians 12:8–10, Paul's words,

> Three times I pleaded with the Lord to take it away from me. But he said to me, "My grace is sufficient for you, for my power is made perfect in weakness." Therefore I will boast all the more gladly

about my weaknesses, so that Christ's power may rest on me. That is why, for Christ's sake, I delight in weaknesses, in insults, in hardships, in persecutions, in difficulties. For when I am weak, then I am strong.

Although I have suffered physically because of losing my child to suicide, I know I can rest in the able everlasting arms of my Heavenly Father, that He is acquainted with grief, that He's fully in control, and that He loves and delights in me, as unworthy as I am. I cling to my Rock, and He daily meets me. Psalm 18:2–6, 16–19,

> The Lord is my rock, my fortress and my deliverer;
> my God is my rock, in whom I take refuge,
> my shield and the horn of my salvation, my stronghold.
> I called to the Lord, who is worthy of praise,
> and I have been saved from my enemies.
> The cords of death entangled me;
> the torrents of destruction overwhelmed me.
> The cords of the grave coiled around me;
> the snares of death confronted me.
> In my distress I called to the Lord;
> I cried to my God for help.
> From his temple he heard my voice;
> my cry came before him, into his ears.
> He reached down from on high and took hold of me;
> he drew me out of deep waters.
> He rescued me from my powerful enemy,
> from my foes, who were too strong for me.
> They confronted me in the day of my disaster,
> but the Lord was my support.
> He brought me out into a spacious place;
> he rescued me because he delighted in me.

Chapter 7

WHY?

In my online grief group for parents who have lost a child to suicide, one of the details we almost universally share is that none of us saw it coming. The only ones who thought it might one day happen were those whose children had already tried and failed in the past. Most of us were blindsided. Even as we saw Trevor unraveling, even as I saw the look of relief on his face as he carefully carried his borrowed shotgun into the house, even as he talked about needing to spill his blood before "they" got into the house or they would hurt us, too, even then, I didn't believe for a second that he would actually take his life. That was something foreign to me. Parents don't anticipate that their child, that baby they held in their arms, that toddler tossing sand on the beach, that child with banged knees after trying those roller skates for the first time, that teenager who perfected the eye roll so masterfully, that young adult who seemed to be finally finding his way in the world, that this dear child would quietly exit the world and leave behind a warehouse full of questions. We torture ourselves trying to answer the unanswerable. Johns Hopkins University states, "Most people who commit suicide have a mental disorder, most commonly a depressive disorder or a substance use disorder."[23]

I saw a video by the Norwich City Football Club about mental health awareness. It depicts two men who regularly attend football games together. Throughout the season, one is always cheerful and upbeat, while the other seems despondent, clapping with no enthusiasm, often remaining seated while the other fans stand and cheer wildly. The quiet man answers questions such as how his week had gone with short, clipped responses. The energetic friend tries to engage with him to little avail. At the end of the video, the quiet man comes alone to the game. He places his friend's scarf on the empty seat next to him. The caption across the screen reads, "At times, it can be obvious when someone is struggling to cope." It fades out, and another caption appears, "but sometimes the signs are harder to spot."[24] In my online group, we discuss often how well our children hid their distress. Some of them could have won Academy Awards with their happy antics and seeming love of life, while behind their closed bedroom doors their anguish spilled out in journals to be found only once it was too late. I think we all have to admit, too, that if signs were there, we missed them. We were in denial that our child could actually carry out that permanent solution to a temporary problem. It couldn't possibly happen in real life. That was the plot of made-for-TV movies. Maybe it could happen rarely in some city in another state. It certainly wouldn't happen in our city, much less our neighborhood, or, unspeakably, in our own house. But it did. Why? Nemours Children's Health says,

> Most teens interviewed after making a suicide attempt say that they did it because they were trying to escape from a situation that seemed impossible to deal with or to get relief from really bad thoughts or feelings. They didn't want to die as much as they wanted to escape from what was going on. And at that particular moment dying seemed like the only way out.[25]

For many who have taken their lives, it seems that they didn't actually want to die. They just didn't want to live with their inescapable pain anymore. If mental illness is the most common reason behind suicides, it's crucial to try to understand why it seems to be increasing in recent years. Health.com poses possible reasons for the escalating prevalence of mental illness, including social media use, increased isolation "due to societal trends like decreased community involvement and fewer people getting married and having children," and lack of access to care.[26] The American Psychological Association has found, "The percentage of young Americans experiencing certain types of mental health disorders has risen significantly over the past decade, with no corresponding increase in older adults."[27] They attribute this to cultural changes over the last decade, such as the use of electronic communication, peer pressure through social media platforms, and the indication that young people are sleeping fewer hours per night than past generations did. The National Institutes of Health, as well as numerous other sources, points out the correlation between substance abuse and suicide.[28]

These answers to the agonizing "why," though, don't really bring any comfort. As I ponder my son's mental illness and my inability to help him, I feel no comfort, no ah-ha moments, and no relief.

My friend Carol shared with me a scripture that helped her tremendously. Psalm 139:16 says, "Your eyes saw my unformed body; all the days ordained for me were written in your book before one of them came to be." Our sons' days were numbered from the time they were born. How their lives ended might have depended on their choices or the choices of others, but the number of their days was set. God did not take our children from us before the appointed time. Along with Carol, I find great comfort in that scripture.

As I thought about the number of Trevor's days already being known by the God who created him, I had to consider the painful thought that perhaps God Himself caused Trevor to take his own life. Is that possible? Would a loving God do that? Did God orchestrate all the details of the month leading up to the horrible day? This is approaching something far bigger than I. As I've battled with that, I've concluded that I do believe God orchestrated what happened, the way it all unfolded. Only God knows for sure, but that fits with what I know of God. Steve and I believe that God lovingly took Trevor home, relieving his deep suffering once and for all. The timing of my dad coming to know God and Trevor returning to faith was fresh in our minds. Was this God's gracious way of preparing us for the depth of grief to come? Were the vehicles that pulled up outside our house part of God's plan to rescue our tormented son? As we talked to his friends extensively in the following months, it became clear that much of what Trevor thought simply wasn't true. No one thought he was a snitch. We know now that there was no gang by the name he told me. But the trap of his mental illness held a firm grasp on him, a grip that was never likely to loosen. Maybe a better question than 'would a loving God do this' would be 'would a loving God NOT do this?' As I reflect on all that happened, I have to think that God allowed us to taste His mercy by not only allowing The Event, but perhaps even causing it Himself. Dr. David Powlison says,

> . . .your significant sufferings don't happen by accident. There's no random chance. No purposeless misery. No bad luck. Not even (and understand this the right way) a tragedy. *Tragedy* means ruin, destruction, downfall, an unhappy ending with no redemption.

Why?

> Your life story may contain a great deal of misery and heartache along the way. But in the end, in Christ, your life story will prove to be a *comedy* in the original sense of the word, a story with a happy ending. You play a part in the *Divine Comedy*, as Dante called it, with the happiest ending of any story ever written. Death, mourning, tears, and pain will be no more (Rev. 21:4). Life, joy, and love get last say. High sovereignty is going somewhere.[29]

"Are not two sparrows sold for a penny? Yet not one of them falls to the ground outside your Father's care" (Matthew 10:29). I have found that I can more than accept that. I can embrace it.

When our senior pastor returned to the U.S. a few days after The Event, he made a visit to us a priority. Steve told him that he had some theological questions. Our pastor, also named Steve, listened carefully and patiently. He shared several pertinent scriptures with us, but the one that best satisfied our hearts was Deuteronomy 29:29, "The secret things belong to the Lord our God, but the things revealed belong to us and to our children forever, that we may follow all the words of this law." Steve the pastor, at Steve the husband's request, wrote in my husband's Bible next to the Deuteronomy passage a short summary of his wise words as he sat with us, ministering to our hearts, counseling us, and praying with us. He wrote, "Remember to focus on what we do know and that is full of grace in Trevor's story. What we don't know is in the shadows–and those secrets belong to God and to our children forever." We resolved to rest in that wise counsel and to accept that God doesn't mean us to understand the depths of all of the difficult things of this life. We will embrace what God has allowed. We will trust that He will use it somehow to His own glory. We can go on without knowing all the why's. We need to let go. We have let go.

Chapter 8

BELONGINGS

We had had to empty Trevor's apartment quickly, but now with no energy and cringing to even think about what to do with any of it, the best we could do was consolidate. Hayley took a few items, but the rest was piled in our garage and in every room of our downstairs. Gradually, we moved all the boxes into the dining room and tried to combine similar things into a smaller number of boxes. Trevor loved plants, and his many lush pots of greenery filled in every gap between my own plants. I looked at them with mixed feelings, loving their beauty, but dreading taking care of them. My son was. . . I couldn't say it. I couldn't let that happen to his beloved plants. I had to keep them alive.

After the memorial service, Steve and I agreed that we should slowly start going through Trevor's boxes and deciding what to do with everything. A few of his friends had requested specific pieces of clothing, mainly jackets that reminded them of him. We gladly gifted those items and quickly realized that the first things we needed to deal with were the rest of his clothing. He had been a smoker and vaper. The odors from those, as well as from Bill, the smelly cat, permeated every item of clothing. Devastated, I laundered it all, destroying the bad odors, but also eliminating the scent of my son. We each chose some pieces we loved, shirts and coats that held memories. I did some online searching for where to donate the rest. I couldn't bear the thought of dropping it all in a thrift store donation bin. It seemed disrespectful to Trevor. In my searching, I came across an organization here in Richmond that helps men and women who are trying to get back on their feet. Caritas[30] began in the 1980s as an all-volunteer project to provide a place to sleep for the homeless. Churches across the city participated in providing cots, showers, and meals. Eventually, the organization grew and obtained a permanent home, a facility large enough to house the people they were seeking to help and to provide instruction and support for those trying to recover from addiction and other problems, including mental illness. I called them and asked if they accepted donations. Yes, they did, and they would be grateful for anything I could provide. Trevor would have been pleased to know his clothing would be helping people with struggles similar to his own. One of Steve's coworkers lost her son a year after we lost Trevor, and we learned that he had stayed at Caritas for some time. I told Steve's coworker, as we hugged and talked about our losses, that her son might have worn one of our son's shirts, that it was almost like her son getting a hug from Trevor. It was an odd connection, but a comforting one.

A few small pieces of furniture found spots in our house, but most of it needed to be re-homed. I posted a few pieces in our neighborhood "Buy Nothing" group, and people came to cart away shelving units and various odds and ends. His desk, though, we had to think about. He had loved that desk. We had gotten it second hand when he was a young teenager, a large and sturdy wood unit. He used that desk constantly. He sat there to do schoolwork, to compose music, to practice his guitar, to play video games, and to sit and read with his feet up on top of it. Of all his furniture, the desk was the only piece he had kept through every move he made, at least six different places he had lived. The desk would be hard to let go. It held precious memories. How would we ever be able to just send it off with a stranger? Reluctantly, I posted it online. It was listed as free, but I requested that people tell me a few things about the intended recipient. Ten people responded, but nine of them just clicked the "is this still available" button. Only one told me something about the person she wanted it for. She wanted it for her seven-year-old son, who loves Legos and Minecraft. That was a start, but not enough. I looked at her personal page, where I could see her public posts. The first one showed a donation to a Suicide and Crisis Lifeline. I cried and thanked my Lord for providing someone I could let this precious desk go to. I pulled out a drawer and wrote with a permanent marker on the bottom, putting Trevor's name and wishing the new owner many years of creativity at his new desk. I didn't tell the woman and her husband why Trevor no longer needed it, but as they loaded it up, she kept glancing at my face, and even though I tried to hold myself together, she put the pieces together. As they tied the final rope on their pickup, she turned and thanked me, and I burst into tears. She held me and told me they would be praying for us. How hard it was to see that symbol of Trevor be carted away. One more task was completed, hundreds more tears released.

One of the numerous boxes in the dining room held Trevor's pots and pans. He had nice kitchen equipment, being an aspiring chef, nicer than what I owned, but I couldn't bring myself to use his, at least, not yet. One day they might bring me joy to use. I would hang onto them, still boxed up. We sorted through and put paperwork with paperwork, artwork with artwork, and electronics and cords together. It took months of working bit by bit, but we finally sorted out books, DVDs, and old VHS tapes, choosing some to keep and the rest to donate. Trevor's remaining belongings were harder to deal with. We were down to things we didn't want to just toss away, but we didn't know what to do with them. My dad passed away three months after Trevor. It took several months before my sister and I were ready to go through his room, but when we finally did, I realized that I now had a place to put the rest of Trevor's boxes. There was no rule for how quickly we had to complete the job. I wasn't ready to use or to get rid of many of his things. We agreed that out of sight would work for now, and my dad's room became the place to store Trevor's boxes until we decided what to do with them.

As a musician, Trevor had quite a few electronics other than instruments. A musician friend at church who works as a media and production engineer offered to look at what we had and give us an idea of whether it was worth anything. Chris' help enabled us to get into the mindset of actually selling some things. He gave us an idea of how much we might reasonably ask for various pieces, and I got to work listing them. We had initially thought we couldn't possibly sell Trevor's things and make a profit from his leaving, but at this point, we agreed that it was fitting to use money from his belongings to pay for expenses related to him. I thought to myself as I met people at the Safe Exchange Zone at our local courthouse, "Trevor, we're going to get you a nice headstone. It won't be flashy, because you weren't flashy, but it will be just right for you." Each item I sold was a relief, and each sale also brought me to tears as I drove away. I didn't want to be designing a headstone. I wanted my son!

I came up with a plan for the box of thousands of tiny items that had been dumped from his desk drawers. I purchased a two-gallon glass jar with a lid, and on the one-year anniversary of losing him, we went through that box. We actually chose to acknowledge that date the day before, on

Belongings

Saturday, instead of the actual day, Sunday. Since it had happened on a Saturday, that Saturday felt like the actual anniversary. The job took us hours. We started by lighting a candle and reading scripture and praying together. As we were doing that, a lovely plant arrived at our door from the staff at church, remembering us and Trevor and letting us know they were praying for us. How precious again our church family was to us! The timing was God's, with the plant arriving just as we finished praying and before we opened the challenging box we had committed to sorting through. That loving remembrance helped to steady us for the task before us. When we were ready, we solemnly opened the stuffed box. We pulled out one item at a time, both of us looking at it and deciding together what to do with it. Some things needed to go into the trash. Some things, such as paperwork, ended up in other boxes. The rest, one treasured item at a time, went gently into the jar. We found ticket stubs, including a few for concerts Steve and Trevor had attended together, birthday and Christmas cards I had sent him over the years, bottle caps and corks, stickers he had designed, pieces of wood he had whittled, artist's tools, a sewing kit I had given him, string, cat toys, spray paint can nozzles, and even the paint chip card from when we painted his bedroom orange. We put the jar of treasures in a spot upstairs where most people who come into our house won't see it. Those who do notice it will be those who know us well enough to be in the upstairs of our home, and they'll understand what that jar means to us. It wouldn't bother me for anyone at all to see it, but we understand that some people don't know what to say and would be uncomfortable with it sitting out in obvious sight.

Dealing with belongings doesn't seem to end. Years ago, I sorted out all the things each child had stuffed into our attic. I threw out things that were obviously trash, like old candy wrappers. Then I packed each child's belongings into large plastic storage tubs and labeled them with their names. Trevor had the most. I haven't figured out how or when to deal with those. They can wait. One day, the grandkids reminded me I had told them that Uncle Stephen and Uncle Trevor had lots of Legos in my attic. They jumped up and down in front of me, grinning and begging me to get them out. I acquiesced to getting out Trevor's, not explaining that there was no longer a reason to save them. He would never have his own children to pass them on to. As the kids sprawled across the floor pawing through Trevor's Legos, squealing with delight as they came across Star Wars pieces and special bricks, I fought back tears. I usually didn't care if others saw me cry, but I didn't want the kids to ever know how hard it was to see them playing with Trevor's Legos. His Legos were now theirs.

The coffee mug I had frantically hidden from Trevor so he wouldn't take it back to his apartment became the one I used daily. For a year, I used it regularly. After the year anniversary, it suddenly ceased to be a comfort and became painful to even look at. I'm not sure why that is. I suppose it's a normal part of grieving in some way. I shoved it to the back of the cabinet, but I expect that at some point, it will return to the front. I don't have to analyze and understand why my emotions change as I continue to move through grief. Sometimes, thinking through those changes can help, but sometimes I need to just let go and stop dissecting my thoughts. I can simply respond however I need to.

In addition to Trevor's belongings, we had to deal with our own. The repair work on our bedroom took weeks before I was able to get in and finally see it. Steve said that if I was willing, he wanted to leave it completely in my hands. He preferred not to be part of setting our bedroom back up. It was too emotional, more than he wanted to handle along with working full-time, and he knew that I could do it. I was fine with that.

I first entered on a quiet day after breakfast while Steve was at work. The walls and carpeting were pretty, and the new window shades, accordion style, could stand alone without the curtains that had been discarded. I needed this room to be completely different if we were ever to sleep in there again. I gazed at the room, with only two pieces of furniture left in it, the larger pieces that the carpet team had kindly repositioned for me. I opened the closet door to find it packed full of giant heavy-weight plastic bags stuffed with our belongings. Even the trinket shelves from the walls were in the bags along with all the trinkets and whatever a worker had picked up and tossed in with them. The bathroom was stacked in every corner with piles of books, lamps, boxes of the grandkids' toys, pictures from the walls, the TV set, small furniture pieces, necklaces I had had hanging on a wall all jumbled in a tangled mess, stacks of DVD's, gift wrap that had been stored under our bed, all heaped in unorganized piles. Even the shower held a pile of books. I parked myself on the floor, prayed, and thought. I had a job ahead of me.

I started with the closet, pulling out a bag at a time. It took only a few minutes to realize that as kind and compassionate as the workers were, their actual work left much to be desired. They had not cleaned well. I would need to wipe down every item. Many items were fine, but I wanted to take no chances. I needed to be sure that there were no traces of anything anywhere. I worked for an hour or two at a time, then took a break and spent time with my dad, attending to his needs and reading to him. I ordered new things for the bedroom, keeping receipts as the insurance company had instructed. My glider rocker had been discarded. I decided to get twin glider rockers to replace it. I got rid of some smaller furniture pieces just to make it a different place. I rearranged, adding twinkle lights on a timer that would come on next to our glider rockers, winding up around a floor lamp that had been Trevor's. I installed heavy plant brackets above each window and hung plants instead of replacing the curtains. Most of the things that had been on the walls went elsewhere, either donated or discarded. Only a few small things would now be on the walls. I searched for a new comforter and found one I thought we would both like. And finally the day came, a week before the memorial service, when the new bed would arrive. I nervously anticipated sleeping in our room again that night. But the truck broke down and the bed couldn't be delivered. They rescheduled for a few days later. Two strong men carried it in, only to find that one leg was damaged. They had to leave the bed unassembled and take back the damaged piece. It wouldn't be delivered until a few days after the memorial service. We would remain in our makeshift beds in the living room.

The next week, with many apologies, the company brought the replacement piece and finished setting up the bed. I put the new bedding on it, vacuumed the carpet, and closed the door. I asked several close friends to be praying about our first night back in our bedroom, that we wouldn't have nightmares or flashbacks. When Steve got home from work, the sun was setting and the bedroom was lit only by the twinkle lights. Steve entered the bedroom for the first time since The Event and gasped. He looked at me, wide-eyed, and said, "This is a holy place!" It was what I had prayed God would make it for us, a sanctuary, a positive place to remember and grieve, and not a sorrowful, grim reminder. We sat down in the two glider rockers and talked about Trevor. Steve's eyes traveled the room and he again stated that this was a holy place. It was a holy place, he said, because this was where Trevor had entered the arms of Jesus. In hindsight, I was glad the bed had been delayed. It was easier to move into the next phase of figuring out how life would look now, of having our bedroom back, with the memorial service behind us. God has carried us through every single part of this horrendous journey, down to the details of having the bed delayed not once, but twice! We could focus on what was next instead of still being preoccupied with the details of the memorial service and interment. That night, we slept, and we slept well. Neither of us has had a single nightmare, not that night and not any night since. We've both had a few dreams with Trevor in them, but in every one of them, he's been at about age eight to eleven. Maybe that's because he was so happy during those years, and that's how we try to remember him the most. I couldn't have predicted how God would make our bedroom a place where we would not only be comfortable again, but truly enjoy being. Every night when Steve gets home from work, we sit in our bedroom to debrief our days. It's become a tranquil, peaceful place of comfort for us. God answered my prayers about that room far more meaningfully than I had even imagined. Thank you, Lord!

    I submitted all the receipts for replacing the bedroom items that had to be destroyed. The insurance company called and told me I had misunderstood, that only the physical structure was covered. Our belongings weren't covered. I'm certain that that's not what I was told. I even had an official document on which to list everything. But the person covering our claim was suddenly no longer available. I read our policy, and they were correct. It seems that the original person had advised us incorrectly. We weren't going to argue with them. Our policy should cover what we've paid for it to cover, no more and no less. Steve and I sighed, a bit frustrated, but we shrugged our shoulders. We had seen God provide in the past. He would provide again.

Chapter 9

SIGNS

Oh, how we longed for one more hug, one more laugh, one more conversation, even one more eye roll from Trevor. I think it's natural for parents who have lost a child, or actually, anyone who has lost someone dear, to want to see some sort of evidence that their loved one is okay. A quick online search will bring up scores of sites discussing how loved ones send signs from Heaven in the forms of cardinals, coins, butterflies, feathers, and other assorted things. In my online grief group, many people talked about wanting to have a medium contact their child to alleviate their worries and grief. I'm grateful that God steered us far away from that sort of thinking from the very start. I have relatives who have attested to how their loved ones communicated from beyond. Years ago, puzzled, I asked my husband what he thought about those claims, some of which seemed to have merit because of the details involved. His wise and scriptural response was that we don't know where those things came from. We're fighting a spiritual battle, and minions of evil are able to trick us into thinking we're getting a message from a loved one or even from God Himself, when we're really being deceived. People who try to contact their loved ones via a medium are opening themselves up to realms of the spiritual world that we're warned against. Scripture speaks to the use of mediums in many passages, both in the old and the new testaments. Leviticus 19:31, "Do not turn to mediums or seek out spiritists, for you will be defiled by them. I am the Lord your God." Isaiah 8:19–20, "When someone tells you to consult mediums and spiritists, who whisper and mutter, should not a people inquire of their God? Why consult the dead on behalf of the living? Consult God's instruction and the testimony of warning. If anyone does not speak according to this word, they have no light of dawn." Acts 16:16–19, in which a woman with an evil spirit who predicts the future has that spirit called out of her by Paul in the name of Jesus, to the dismay of the woman's owners, who were making considerable money from her spirit of evil. 2 Kings 21:6, "[Mannasseh] sacrificed his own son in the fire, practiced divination, sought omens, and consulted mediums and spiritists. He did much evil in the eyes of the Lord, arousing His anger." 1 Timothy 4:1, "The Spirit clearly says that in later times some will abandon the faith and follow deceiving spirits and things taught by demons." 1 Chronicles 10:13, "Saul died because he was unfaithful to the Lord; he did not keep the word of the Lord and even consulted a medium for guidance, and did not inquire of the Lord." 2 Corinthians 11:14, ". . .Satan himself masquerades as an angel of light." There are many other passages, as well. Since we had already thought through the receiving of signs and personal contact from beyond, we were spared the torment of having to work through that on top of the intensity of our grief. I suspect that if we had opened ourselves up to seeking signs, we might have "seen" some. Many claim to have seen signs sent by their loved ones, those coins or creatures in nature that are all too often attributed to being messages or messengers. But how can we know where those signs are from, or if they're even signs at all? Do our missing loved ones long to communicate with us? Can they even see us from Heaven? Scripture is unclear about this. In addressing this question, John Piper looks at Hebrews 12:1, "Therefore, since we are surrounded by so great a cloud of witnesses, let us also lay aside every weight, and sin which clings so closely, and let us run with endurance the race that is set before us." He concludes,

> But I am inclined to think that it does mean they are watching, partly because of the picture of the race. It is as though the saints finish their marathon at their death. Then they come around and stand on the side of the racetrack and watch us. And we are supposed to take heart from that because, in essence, they would be saying, "Hang in there. Trust God. You can do this. We made it; you can make it too.[31]

Yet even as he acknowledges that our loved ones may be able to see what's going on back here on earth, Piper warns us to be careful not to yield to the temptation to attempt to communicate with the saints in Heaven, but rather to remember that

Christ is the one mediator between God and man. The New Testament does not encourage us to make the saints or Mary into mediators as we seek God's help.[32]

In an article published by The Gospel Coalition, Katie Polski says, in pondering whether her parents in Heaven can see her,

> ... Scripture doesn't give us enough evidence to say for sure.... It could be that the Lord provides glimpses of what's going on in my life.... But we do know that if our loved ones see things on earth, they don't see with the same eyes you and I have because their perspective is no longer tainted by sin.

She goes on to point out that becoming overly focused on whether our loved ones are regularly peeking over our shoulders can misdirect our thoughts.

> This emphasis can lead us to think more about our loved ones and less about Jesus. We might even begin to have more conversations with them than we do with the Lord.[33]

Maybe Trevor sees us. Maybe not. As I wonder about that, I have also to consider whether I even want him to. Wouldn't it be much better for him to be basking in our Lord, communing with the patriarchs of the faith, and creating new music for his face-to-face worship with God? Would I prefer for him to be focusing on what's happening in this broken world he's no longer a part of? Further, a deeper question than if I really want Trevor to be seeing us is whether I actually need him to. Can I let go of that? I have God, who is all-powerful, omniscient, wise, and completely loving, as an Anchor for my soul. Do I expect that Trevor can give me something that God can't? Trevor is with the Lord. He no longer has to check in with me. I loved him deeply, and I know he loved me. Seeing a sign won't change that. Tim Challies, who lost his twenty-one-year-old son, notes,

> Our loved ones cross the river and are lost to our sight and our hearts burn to know that they have passed over safely. It is natural, then, to hope for some kind of information, to seek some kind of a sign, to know that they are okay.
>
> But even in the absence of a sign, I am convinced that Nick is okay. In fact, I am convinced that he is better than okay—he is the best he has ever been. Though death has for a time separated him from this world, it has transported him to the presence of God. In the moment he left here, he entered there. In the instant he arrived in heaven all trace of sin and its effects were obliterated so that he no

longer sins or even wants to and no longer suffers or even can. His faith has become sight.[34]

Considering that we don't know where a perceived sign came from, that bird flitting around, or a coin dropped in an unusual place, Steve and I would prefer not to look for signs. A young dad, Austin DeArmond, who lost a young son, wrote in his blog about another aspect of the signs that many look for, observing that

> Believing in these 'signs' could lead to greater pain when the butterfly is eaten or the bird gets hit by a car. There's an arbitrariness or selectivity to this line of reasoning which betrays its logic altogether. Is my son in the wind when tornados take other human lives or just when it feels good upon my cheek? Is he the rain when it mists slowly outside or also when it becomes a monsoon and drowns? Is he sending rainbows after a calming rainstorm but not responsible when the levees break and destruction ensues? Is he sending birds to me when they're eating out of my bird feeder by my window but not when they're tearing apart other living things squirming around on the ground?[35]

I don't believe that Trevor has suddenly received the ability to control nature to send us signs, nor do I believe that such would be his focus. If he sees us from Heaven, he sees that our faith is in God and that we don't need questionable signs to bolster that faith. Perceived signs of unknown origin would only serve to unsettle us.

Our God, though, is gentle and merciful to us. He knows our heartache. He provides for us in countless ways. My friend Carol gave me the perfect word for those times when God provides some sort of connection, unlooked for and timed perfectly for our wounded hearts. She calls those times "assurances." There's a difference between signs from our loved ones and an assurance from God.

I've had two assurances. I did not pray for them, and I did not expect them, but God blessed me to the point of actual tears, tears of both grief and gratitude as He brought my focus to Himself. The first time was only about a week after The Event. I had read the Psalms for a while and was immersed in prayer. I was worshipping and focusing on His attributes, the things that make Him and Him alone God. It was one of those particularly deep worship times, and I was completely engulfed in wonder and awe of God, losing all awareness of anything going on around me. Suddenly in my mind my hand went up in a wave and I said internally, "Hi Trevor!" How exceedingly bizarre that was! That unbidden thought startled me, giving me a physical jolt, and breaking me down into tears as I reflected on Trevor, whole and healthy and full of joy as he sat at the very feet of his Savior in Heaven. My response could be nothing other than continuing to worship once I collected myself from the shock, with the peace of the assurance that my son was in much better hands than mine. The second assurance was when I went back to church for the first time. I had missed five Sundays. After Trevor's interment, I felt the need to get back into some sort of normalcy. For me, Sunday mornings include rehearsal and two services as I sit in my little place of serving, running the software that projects media on the wall, including song lyrics and videos. I had no energy as I woke up that morning, and my heart wanted both to stay in bed and to be back in church. I found jeans and a more or less unwrinkled shirt to wear rather than my usual dressy church attire, unable to muster the strength necessary to match up and prepare my prettier clothes, even for the Lord. The Lord knew my heart. Just going to be with His people was the important part. Steve graciously stayed home with my dad as I headed to church. As I reached the top of our driveway, I looked to the left for cars before I pulled out, and there, perfectly centered over the end of our street, was a stunning rainbow. It had not rained! The rainbow stayed in my field of vision for the entire half hour drive to church, no matter which way my car turned. The glorious hymn by Thomas Chisholm "Great Is Thy Faithfulness"[36] expresses it far better than my own words:

>Great is Thy faithfulness, O God my Father
>
>There is no shadow of turning with Thee
>
>Thou changest not, Thy compassions, they fail not
>
>As Thou hast been, Thou forever will be
>
>Great is Thy faithfulness
>
>Great is Thy faithfulness
>
>Morning by morning new mercies I see
>
>All I have needed Thy hand hath provided
>
>Great is Thy faithfulness, Lord, unto me
>
>Summer and winter and springtime and harvest
>
>Sun, moon and stars in their courses above
>
>Join with all nature in manifold witness

Circle of Sorrow

To Thy great faithfulness, mercy and love.

I had prayed as I pulled out of the garage that God would help me to handle the inevitable tears, hugs, words of encouragement, and love from my church family. I both dreaded and desperately needed every hug offered! Watching that amazing rainbow as I drove to church that morning assured my heart yet again of God's tender love and mercy to me. Tim Challies points out that God can and does provide circumstances such as rainbows to encourage us through difficult times. He clarifies the difference between a sign from our loved one versus circumstances arranged providentially by God, saying,

> surely these ought to be understood as God expressing his love and care, not our loved ones intervening in the world. It's *God's* presence that is meant to comfort us, not the possible presence of those we have loved and lost.[37]

I treasure the assurances that God has given me, and I can confidently say that I neither expect nor want signs from Trevor. He has other things to do, things of which I can only dream right now. I wouldn't want him to be doing anything else!

Chapter 10

MILESTONES

I had always heard that the first year is the hardest after a deep loss. As significant dates come up–birthdays, holidays, days important to the family–the absence of that one person casts a pall over the day. I've had other losses, but not like this one where every milestone wrenched my battered heart. We knew we'd need to figure out how to handle each of those milestones in the future. Initially, though, we would have to simply encounter them and muddle through as best we could. We weren't ready to mull over how to recognize those dates well.

For me, each and every day was a milestone. After a week, I realized it had been seven days. Then it had been ten days, then fourteen days, then thirty. I found myself knowing exactly how many days it had been for over a year. At nine months, I realized he had been gone for the same amount of time I had carried him in my womb, and I wept. My baby, that sweet child, was gone. I found myself lost in memories of that pregnancy and his birth. I felt him in my arms, tiny and healthy, and treasured the memories of thousands of kisses on his little nose. All those middle-of-the-night feedings, so long ago, were precious times with just the two of us.

I was avoiding social media, mostly because it seemed so frivolous. My child had died! I didn't care about the funny meme someone had found, or the corrected grammar on someone's post (even though they needed to hear it), or the photos of someone's BBQ. I did occasionally post. I posted about Trevor's desk. I posted his memorial video on his birthday. At the six-month mark, which felt like a milestone, I wrote a somewhat lengthy post about what we had learned and about how grateful we were for the

Circle of Sorrow

many who had surrounded us right after The Event and then ongoing. A number of people told me after I posted that I should write a book. In my journal, I wrote about how I had been told that I'm a wordsmith and that I have a story to tell. I wrote that I'm no wordsmith, and I'm certainly not wordy enough to write a whole book. I don't have earth-shaking insights. There are already lots of books out there on the subject. But I told them they could pray about it, and we'd see what God does. I ended that journal entry with "It's not likely I'll ever write a book." But I prayed about it, too, and as time went on, I slowly realized that although there are many books about grief, there are very few about losing a child to suicide, especially from a first-person Christian perspective. A window cracked open to the possibility. It cracked open a bit further when, a few months later, as we sat together in our glider rockers debriefing our days, Steve listened to my thoughts about how my river had been that day and things I felt like God was teaching me. He told me he thought I needed to write a book. He's not on social media and had not been aware that others had suggested that or that I had been praying about it. I prayed more earnestly, becoming more open to the possibility.

Trevor's birthday is in the middle of October, seven weeks after he left and three weeks after his burial. Steve and I spent the afternoon at the cemetery, reading and praying. Our tears watered the sad grass above his body. There was nothing cathartic, healing, or cleansing in that day. It was a day to somehow just get through. If the bottle in which God holds our tears were a literal bottle, the volume in it would have risen by at least an inch that day. Back home again, our heavy hearts dragged through each hour, and I was grateful to escape into sleep that night.

My dad passed away the Sunday before Thanksgiving that year, outliving his grandson by three months. I mourned his loss, but it paled in comparison to losing Trevor. My dad was ninety-four years old and had accepted Jesus as his Savior as he lay on his hospice bed. He was ready, and his departure from this world was a mercy to him. I pictured him reuniting with Trevor, and that brought me a measure of joy. While my dad was still with us, I had been continuing with my Friday morning Bible study by Facetiming in. As they prepared to start, one of the women would call me, then set the phone in the middle of the table so I could hear them. It wasn't ideal, but it connected me. Those women heard my anguish a multitude of times, and they patiently let me talk when I needed to, always ready with prayer and with an encouraging word. I texted them during times when I felt like I was drowning, and they bolstered me up every single time. Gradually, their identity to me changed from being my Friday morning Bible study group to being My Girls. I cherish that group! When Thanksgiving came, we were invited to join in with others, but we weren't up to it. It was the first major holiday, and we needed to be alone to work through it. My Girls jumped into action and provided us with an entire Thanksgiving meal. With my dad's bed upstairs now empty, the house seemed especially quiet as we sat in our kitchen to eat that special meal and to think back over the year. We knew we had more to be thankful for than we could possibly understand, our gracious God holding us up and providing in so many ways. My life verse has long been 1 Thessalonians 5:16–18, "Rejoice always, pray continually, give thanks in all circumstances, for this is God's will for you in Christ Jesus." Often, we aren't sure what God's will for us is in this or that situation, but we know that giving thanks is always God's will. During times of stress in the past, I've sometimes sat down and just given thanks. Initially, it would be easy, going to all the obvious things, like my family, a roof over our heads, and food to eat. But after a while, I would reach into the nitty gritty things, the small things or the deeper things, and especially the hard things, knowing that God uses those times to help us draw closer to Him and find the rest we need. As Steve and I sat over our Thanksgiving dinner, we talked, we cried, and we poured out thanks to our God, who hasn't made us puppets, who allows all of us to make choices, good or bad, and who is then there to carry us through when our choices or the bad choices of others turn our lives in directions we can't handle on our own.

Our church has a Thanksgiving Eve service every year with music and a short message, but a major part of the service is an open mic time for people to share things in their lives for which they're thankful. I've attended every one of those services over the years, running PowerPoint and listening, but I've never shared. I'm an ultra-introvert and would prefer to share quietly with a few friends rather than the entire congregation. This year was different. I strongly wanted to thank my church for surrounding us as they had. I thought carefully about what I should say, gathering myself together, ready and confident that I could say what I needed to express. The mic was handed to me, and I began, "This year has been the hardest time either Steve or I has ever had." Then I burst into tears. What I wanted to say quickly changed as I blurted out a weepy, "We cry a lot." I wanted to crawl back into the sound booth and hide, but it was too late, and I needed to express my thanks. I took a few deep breaths so I could continue. "The way that it all unfolded made it so clear that God was in control. We've seen God's grace and mercy to us daily, and this church, Stony Point Church, has loved us well. Thank you," I said to them all as I turned, looking in each direction. "Thank you!" It was succinct, but it was enough. I was sure there were many who had contributed in some way to our needs, especially in prayer, of whom I was unaware. I longed to thank them, and I especially wanted to praise our God by recognizing how He had been carrying us daily, through every painful step of this journey.

As Christmas approached, our daughter suggested that we all converge on an AirBnB about an hour away rather than gathering in our homes, where Trevor's absence would be excruciatingly obvious. We all agreed, and she ran with it, taking charge of all the details. How she found the energy to do all she did is beyond me, but I was grateful. I felt deep relief that we could be someplace else as we tried to figure out how Trevor would somehow still be a part of these important holidays. That insightful plan, though, didn't go as we had all hoped. The week before, both grandchildren were sick. It was more than a cold, but less than the flu. They didn't have fevers or vomiting, just felt extremely weak and overall yucky. For Christmas, they had completely recovered but, unfortunately, had passed it on to both of their parents and to Steve and me. We dragged ourselves to the AirBnB, excited for all of us to be together for Christmas, minus Trevor, but mostly wanting to lie down and sleep our illnesses away. Stephen, traveling from Denver, texted to inform us that his flight was delayed, and he might not make his connection. His next text told us that his flight had been cancelled altogether and he was scrambling to make other travel arrangements. Between him and Hayley, they managed to call in help from a friend who worked for an airline, used some frequent flyer miles, and got him onto a flight. He arrived in Charlottesville exhausted, but before Christmas. We now had two excited, energetic children, four sick adults, and one completely drained adult in the AirBnB. We tag-teamed taking care of the kids, each adult taking a turn, then heading back to bed. We all managed to be up for Christmas morning, perked up by the kids' happiness, but we quickly fell like lead weights as soon as all the gifts were opened. I had asked Hayley and Stephen if they were okay with Trevor's stocking being hung with all the others. They were, as long as it was taken down when the others came down. I put gift cards into his stocking that I then gave to each adult, one for themselves and another to pass on to anyone they chose in Trevor's memory. It could be a homeless person, a street musician, a friend who needed a shoulder to cry on, or anyone else. It seemed like a good way to remember Trevor, at least for that first Christmas. I would like to say that in spite of sickness, we had a lovely Christmas, but we all felt the enormous tension. The only reason we were in that AirBnB was that Trevor was gone. His absence was more pronounced than we had imagined, more obvious than if we had stayed home, but with the kids always around, we felt we had to avoid any meaningful conversation about it. We continued to take shifts, playing with the kids and then hitting the pillows again. Stephen received text updates about his return flights, also delayed and cancelled, and once again, he had to scramble to find a way to be back at work on time. The plan to go away for that first Christmas was a thoughtful, appropriate one, but we came away all agreeing that we wouldn't do it again.

Then there was Valentine's Day. Who knew that Valentine's Day would be so painful? I hadn't given Valentines to my kids since they were teenagers. But even so, the memories of past Valentine's Days brought the tears to the surface again. I remembered the sweet cards each of the kids had always made every year and the tradition of giving each of them their very own box of chocolates and some other little gift according to their ages at the time. I had thought that Valentine's Day could slip past without twisting my heart around. But no, my heart was not spared. Similarly, the first day of spring came, which had always been a holiday in our home. We did all the Easter-ish stuff on the first day of spring. We colored eggs, got a candy basket, drew pictures of baby chicks, even took the day off from school, since we homeschooled. As a child, I had always thought that was what Easter was, a celebration of spring. As a believing adult, I wanted Easter to be a recognition of Christ's death and resurrection, not a celebration of bunnies, and thus began our first day of spring celebrations. A dear friend whose children had grown up with ours and who had adopted our holiday for her family as well, called that day to check up on me and talk about Trevor. Marilyn has made sure to stay in touch regularly, texting or calling and always willing to talk about my son. It's so vital to know that he's not forgotten. She has ministered to me by being normal, by talking about grief and Trevor, and letting me hear about her life as well, how her children and grandchildren are doing and various family things going on for her. We have a precious friendship that has withstood distance and time. Her calls always make a difference! I don't underestimate the value of normalcy as we chat back and forth about our families and life issues. What a great gift loving conversation is to an aching heart!

Circle of Sorrow

Tax season came. In my online grief group, the subject came up, and as I puzzled over the questions posted, I was shocked to learn that final tax forms had to be filed. Trevor had been single and had no offspring. We were his closest next of kin, so we were responsible for filing his taxes. I gathered together the various papers I needed and sat down to work. I had always done our taxes, not willing to pay someone else to do what I was perfectly capable of doing myself. But this was a new undertaking. I considered hiring someone, but I still would have had to look at all the details and talk to the preparer about it. I didn't think I would be preserving my heart from pain to pay someone else to do it. As I studied the instructions, my frustration increased. The instructions were confusing, not clearly explaining what address to use, whose name to put where, and what additional forms were needed. I needed to call the help line. I couldn't. I sat at my desk, sobbing uncontrollably, emptying a tissue box and grabbing another. I dreaded explaining to a stranger what information I needed and why. I picked up my phone and texted My Girls. They were on it, bathing me with prayer as I made that awful phone call. The woman on the other end sounded like she was in my age range, and she spoke clear English. I wouldn't have to struggle to communicate. She listened carefully, and the first thing she said was to express how sorry she was, followed by assuring me she would make sure I got the answers I needed. She walked me through the unclear parts. Several other forms were needed, and as I pulled them up and looked at them on my computer, she helped me figure out which parts to ignore and which parts to fill out. She came to one part that required help from someone in a different section of the department and needed to transfer me. She told me that she wouldn't put me on hold, that she would keep me on her line until the next person picked up so I wouldn't accidentally be disconnected. Her gentleness with me helped me immeasurably to collect myself and focus. The second person was also a mature-sounding woman who spoke clear English. She, too, expressed sorrow for my loss, then gently walked me through the last portion I needed. When I finally hung up the phone, my brain and my heart were calm. Completing the job would still be tearful. I had to check the box for "deceased." I had to sign his name. I had to sign my own name on forms that weren't mine. But I finally sealed the envelopes and the paperwork went into a drawer, out of sight. Another milestone was behind me.

Then came Mother's Day. My bruised heart felt like a bungee cord was wrapped around it, brutally tight and inescapable. I avoided eye contact as

Milestones

I walked to my spot in the sound booth that Sunday, knowing I was going to collapse in tears with even a glance from anyone. I made it to my seat and proceeded to do all the things that needed doing as though it were a normal Sunday, but my throat was so constricted that I couldn't speak. As in many churches, our church has long been sensitive to the fact that Mother's Day, for some, is an excruciatingly painful day. Some have lost dear mothers, some are mourning that they've never had the joy of being a mother, some experienced abuse at the hands of their mothers and would prefer not to recognize that day, and some, like me, are mothers with hearts bearing the permanent scar of the loss of a child. When the pastor prayed for all the mothers, with joy, but also recognizing the pain for some of us, I couldn't hold back any longer and an ocean came pouring out of my eyes. The service continued, and I sat robotically hitting the keyboard to advance to the next slide as I gasped for air, grateful that the singing drowned out my sobs. I hadn't anticipated that Mother's Day would be the hardest of all the holidays. Friends knew my grief would be especially hard that day, and many came over to quietly hug me, more than a few weeping alongside me. The second Mother's Day proved to be just as hard. Now I know that Mother's Day will always be the hardest special day. On that second Mother's Day, a friend who had lost a young nephew to suicide quietly came around the corner of the sound booth before the first service carrying a vase of beautiful flowers. Her face solemn, she told me she knew it would be a hard day for me and that she was praying for us. That thoughtful gesture and knowing that others were especially praying for me that day helped tremendously. Judy came to me after the service, close to tears already. We wrapped each other in a knowing hug and cried together for our lost sons. We cried for our losses, we cried that they had conditions that couldn't be healed in spite of our efforts, we cried that they didn't get to find the perfect women to marry, we cried that they didn't get to have children and understand for themselves how deeply we love them, we cried that they didn't get to grow in careers, we cried that the world didn't have time to get to know them better. Our tears are never just for our personal loss. There's so much more to grief than that. But yes, many of those tears were simply because we miss our boys. We want one more hug. Hugging each other is as close as we'll get, and I'll cherish every precious hug!

July edged in, and with it, the knowledge that the anniversary was getting close. In July the previous year, Trevor had first reached back out to us, wanting to spend time with each of us individually. We moved through those dates tearfully, recounting what we had done on each of our turns to hang out with him. We had had no idea what was coming during those meals and walks with him. The anniversary of my dad coming to the Lord came, and with it much rejoicing as we thought about how long he had lived without the Lord, and of how the brevity of his life of faith didn't matter. He was with the Lord! Then the anniversary of Trevor calling us in distress and his return to the Lord. Then three days of watching him helplessly as he spiraled down, and the slow realization that he had serious mental illness going on. The anniversary would be on a Sunday. We planned to go to church together and then go to the cemetery. Normally we drove separately, since I needed to arrive in time for worship rehearsal and stayed for both services, but we would go together this time. On Saturday night, Steve changed his mind and decided he needed to sleep a little longer to catch up from his long school week. He would drive separately. I rose early on Sunday morning and got myself ready quietly, letting Steve get the sleep he needed. At the last minute, though, he called downstairs to me that he was up and would go with me. I looked at the time and urged him to hurry. He finally trotted into the kitchen already five minutes past time to leave and headed to the coffee maker. I felt anger rising up as he meandered his way through his morning routine. I took my things out to the car and returned to find him preparing the coffee maker that took six minutes to run instead of the smaller one that took less than two minutes. But first he needed to grind his coffee beans, better, he said, than the already ground stuff we had. My blood boiled as I watched him, tapping my foot. When we finally settled into the car and headed off, my seething anger came out. I yelled at him and told him why I was so angry at him. Those who know me would say, "You yelled? YOU yelled?" Yes, I yelled. The tension of the past year came out in a hot spew of frustration. Steve sat in astonished silence until I finally finished, then apologized profusely. We got to church and went separate ways, me into the sanctuary for rehearsal, and Steve to the library to read and pray. After the service as we headed to the cemetery, he asked how it had gone for me. "Not good," I retorted angrily. He asked why. "Because I missed the first two songs during rehearsal, so in the first song, I didn't know they had changed where the choruses would be, so I didn't correct the PowerPoint and put up the wrong lyrics. And in the second song, there were typos including missing words that I didn't catch." He apologized again, sheepishly. We had managed to get through an entire year with little friction between us as we helped each other through our grief. We made up for it that day. We set up our chairs at Trevor's graveside and talked. We cried for Trevor, we cried for our tension and fighting, we cried for a hundred things. We came planning to read and pray. We were so emotionally exhausted that we finally just sat in silence, listening to the birds and the river noises not far away. We were not figuring out well how to get through these milestones. I hated that. Yet that was also okay. Everyone's grief is different. If we had to simply shuffle through the first year, that's what we would do. There are no right or wrong ways that fit each of us predictably. For the anniversary of Trevor's death, we fought, we made up, we cried, we prayed, and many, many people remembered and hugged us, weeping with us and praying for us.

As we headed into the second year, I asked friends to pray. I had heard that the second year would be easier, but it wasn't starting out that way. I had made it through all the firsts, but I was so numb that I hadn't considered all the seconds, and the thirds, and the tenths. The permanence of this pain became unmistakably real. The depths of my sorrow continued to plague me. I had lost ten pounds and not gained any of it back, despite my concerted efforts. I often had days when I didn't cry, but there was never a day that I wasn't sad. The second birthday that Trevor wouldn't be here for approached, and for the first time, I felt I had a healthy way to embrace a milestone. I purchased a pack of fast-food gift cards, picked up a special breakfast that I wouldn't usually splurge on, grabbed my Psalms journal, and headed to Hollywood Cemetery. It was a sunny fall morning, not yet nippy, as I settled into my chair at Trevor's graveside. We had ordered a headstone for him and were told it would take eight to ten months to make. Unhappy with how long his grave would be unidentified, just a bare patch of grass with no indication that he was even there, I had made him a temporary marker. I bought a large piece of slate-like tile, and using a cutting machine, cut and adhered vinyl text to it. I guess I did okay with it, because a friend whose son is in the same cemetery told me she hadn't realized it wasn't a real headstone when she stopped over to visit my son after visiting her own, until I told her. I prayed and sat quietly listening to nature as I ate an unhurried breakfast. I pulled out my journal and wrote, wrote, wrote. I had remembered to bring a water jug and cleaned the mud off his temporary marker. Next to it, I found the two tiny glass kittens and the swatch of fabric from Anna-Mae and tucked them lovingly into my pocket to bring back once the permanent marker arrived. Finally, I put my chair back in the car and drove to Trevor's old apartment. I had a few of Trevor's stickers with me, and I put several of them on the window above the doorway of his building. It felt a little bit like littering. I won't do it again. But it seemed fitting for the moment. And then I started walking, praying as I went that God would direct my steps. I was seeking homeless people to give my fast-food gift cards to. A vast number of the homeless are in that situation because of mental illness. I felt that giving a tiny help to a few of those suffering like Trevor had would be an appropriate way to honor his memory. I didn't tell any of them why I was giving out gift cards, and I specifically looked for people who weren't panhandling. I wanted to give gift cards to people who weren't expecting anything, just to bless them and provide some practical help. Broad Street can be a little seedy, as a Broad Street probably is in most major cities. It was well-traveled, though, with swarming cars and unceasing foot traffic. I carried my wallet and keys in a small cross-body bag and felt as safe as I ever had in that area of town. I had given out about half of my gift cards when my phone rang. I pulled it out and saw Marilyn's name. I happened to be walking past a small half-wall of brick, and promptly sat down on it to talk with her. She again soothed my wounded heart, not only by listening and talking about Trevor, but by sharing about herself, too, and letting me have normalcy. A loving and refreshing conversation bolstered me to continue my walk. As I crossed the street and circled back, I had a few cards left. I came to a sleeping bag and a basket of personal items in the doorway of a vacant building, clearly someone's claimed spot. I tucked a gift card into the sleeping bag. Finally, having made a large circle, I had one card left as I neared my car. A large man stood on the corner chatting to another who was passing by. As I drew closer, the large man smiled at me, nodded, and told me to have a blessed day. He appeared to be homeless, but it's not always obvious. I smiled back at him and thanked him, handing him the final gift card. His face lit up as he told me he could surely use that and thanked me several times. At last, I had figured out a way to remember Trevor in a special and significant way, a way of which I'm certain he would approve. I can imagine him giving his beautiful chuckle laugh and saying, "Well done, Mom!"

 I began feeling like I could make it through all the other holidays in a more healthy and joyous way now. As the second Christmas crept up, I decided I would actually decorate. The grandkids would be at our house during Christmas break. I wanted the house to look like the Christmases of the past for them. They didn't need to see that our hearts still trembled with pain on some days. I knocked myself out getting the house as merry as I could. Our annual Christmas party with our small group from church needed to be moved to our house unexpectedly, so I dove into a deep clean, knowing that one person is allergic to cats. She insisted that it wasn't a problem, that she'd just take an antihistamine, but I didn't want her to suffer. Steve's brother, who had never visited us in all our years of marriage, said he wanted to come for Christmas, much to Steve's delight. I planned out meals, baked cookies, and came up with some personalized gifts I could make for his brother and a few I could buy. I decided that for Trevor's stocking from now on, I would find some special cat toy for his beloved rescue, Phasma, who was growing in her trust of us and had become surprisingly dear to us, considering that we truly weren't cat people. Everything seemed to be falling into place for a fresh look at Christmas. When the time came for the small group Christmas party, I had everything done except decorating the tree. I had lights on it, but I hadn't been able to carve out the time to open the box of ornaments. That would be tough, as there were so many handmade ornaments from each of the kids, as well as special ornaments that belonged to Trevor. During the party, I realized that the men were all in the living room talking and we women were all in the kitchen. Well, that never happens, does it? I took a deep breath and blurted out, "Hey, y'all wanna help me decorate my tree?" They all expressed enthusiasm, and we trooped into the living room, but only one was able to actually help, while a baby and some physical ailments kept the other women seated but encouraging us from nearby. Valerie helped me carefully unwrap ornaments. She's not only in my small group, but also in my Friday morning Bible study and has been by my side regularly, both physically and in prayer. She blessed me deeply not only by helping, but by how she went about it. She quickly realized that this would be profoundly emotional for me. Every time she unwrapped something that was obviously Trevor's or made by him, she gently handed it to me to place on the tree. Her eyes told me that she was poised to wrap me in a hug if I needed it. She has a flair for decorating, and the tree was lovelier than ever. Valerie's gentle, compassionate help with that vital detail of Christmas enabled me not only to accomplish it, but to be able to look forward to future Christmases with the expectation that I can again tackle that job, and with joy.

Steve's brother arrived a few days before Christmas, and the two of them talked and laughed for hours at a time. I was able to exit and rest as I needed, nursing a cough that had been hanging on for a few weeks. But two days before Christmas as I was preparing dinner, I suddenly felt an intense chill all the way to my bones and an inexplicable weakness. I set a needed pot of water onto the stove to boil and went into the living room to flip on the gas fireplace and huddle in front of it for a few minutes. I might as well have been huddling in front of the refrigerator. Venturing back into the kitchen, I somehow got a pan of manicotti ready, hiding my distress, but the guys said they didn't want to eat for a while yet. I wrote out baking instructions and left them in charge of completing the task, heading upstairs to lie down. I quickly fell asleep, but I woke around four in the morning with shortness of breath. As I lay motionless, yet gasping for air, I knew I needed to head to the ER. I had a dilemma. I knew Steve would immediately get me to the car and sit with me at the ER, but I didn't want his brother to wake up to an empty house. It had taken him too many years to actually visit us, and I didn't want to interrupt the special time they were enjoying together. I decided not to wake my husband up. I was so short of breath it took me an hour to pull on jeans and a sweatshirt and walk to the garage to get in my car. I left a note on the counter in the bathroom so Steve would see it as soon as he woke up. At the ER, I assumed they would give me some antibiotics and send me back home. I might even be back before the guys woke up. I assumed incorrectly. A CT scan showed I had significant pneumonia and they insisted that I had to be admitted to the hospital. Steve found my note and immediately called me, then came and sat with me until I was transferred to the hospital. At that point, I urged him to go back to be with his brother. I was getting IV antibiotics and oxygen and just wanted to sleep. I spent Christmas Eve and Christmas day in the hospital, until the on-call doctor came to see me. I had been told to expect to be in the hospital for four to five days. But as the doctor talked to me, asking how much I was moving around, I expressed how frustrated I was that the nurses weren't letting me get up at all. They were short staffed, and apparently, knowing that I was bed-bound made it easier for them. With the IV and heart monitor leads coming from one side and the oxygen tubing coming from the other, I couldn't even wiggle out of the bed. I knew this because I had tried. As we talked, the doctor saw that I understood what I needed to do to get better. Moving around is important for pneumonia recovery so that secretions in the lungs can be expelled more easily. I didn't even throw into the conversation that I had been a respiratory therapist, although it was on the back burner to bring up if I had to. He agreed to discharge me early as long as I agreed to come right back if I started to get worse. Deal! The IV antibiotics finished flowing into my veins, and he called ahead to my pharmacy so we could pick up oral pills to continue wiping out the infection. Steve and his brother had gone out for a walk, and I couldn't reach them, so Hayley, already planning to come visit me, jumped in her car and quickly came, helped me to her vehicle and got me back home. I spent the next month eating chicken soup and resting. Our scheduled time with the grandkids to give them their gifts at their house had to be postponed, but we did get that a few days after Christmas, staying for only a short time so I wouldn't over-exert myself and land back in the hospital. For the second year in a row, illness kept us from having a new-normal Christmas. There will be more Christmases in our future, unless the Lord wills otherwise. I'm hopeful that for the third one, we'll have continued to progress in our grief journey and will have a strong and hopeful pattern for all the Christmases after that, whatever those may bring. Each new holiday now helps us to rest again in knowing that God has us in His able arms. I've learned that joy and sadness can co-exist. They're both born of love. Joy and grief can hold hands.

In January, I drove to the monument company to ask why Trevor's headstone was taking so long. It had been a full year, not the eight to ten months they had predicted. They treated me with respect and compassion and made phone calls on the spot. I hadn't realized that they don't actually make the headstones themselves. They work with a company who shapes and engraves the stones, then ships them to the monument companies to place on the graves. As they talked with the actual creators of the stones, they were told that Trevor's marker, as well as our own, would probably be finished in March or April and then trucked to Richmond. At least we had an answer, and we would wait. Late in April, we finally got the call. We drove to the cemetery, nervous and uncertain about how this first look at Trevor's actual headstone would be. We both chose scriptures we wanted to read, and I had lyrics to several hymns ready. The workmanship on Trevor's stone made my heart smile. It was beautiful! I stood gazing at it, then heard Steve say, "It's kind of freaky to see our own names on a headstone. At least there isn't a second date on them." I hadn't even glanced at our own stone. Now I stepped over to it and had to agree. It was strange to see my own name in the cemetery. But the focus went back to Trevor's stone, and we brushed a few leaves off it and sat, thinking and praying. Steve said having the headstone finally in place was kind of like putting the period at the end of a sentence. We sang Trevor's favorite hymn, "Holy, Holy, Holy,"[38] and then we sang mine, "It Is Well."[39] That hymn has long been one that I've loved, but in the wake of losing Trevor, it became even more meaningful. The author of that hymn, Horatio Spafford, wrote it after a ship carrying his wife and four daughters sank, with only his wife surviving. Our hearts still hurt, but our souls were indeed well. Butch and Judy were right. It wasn't easier, but this burden was slowly lightening as we carried it with the love and help of God and the many people who had surrounded us.

Back in December, I had arrived home from the hospital and gone straight to bed. I was weak, and, now that I was off oxygen, short of breath with even minimal exertion. Steve's brother headed back home the day after Christmas, and I sat around, limp and sick. It became clear that this recovery would take some time, and I wouldn't be doing anything much more than resting for the duration. I had been praying about whether I should write a book, and once I had felt the call, I decided I needed to wait until after the winter 2023 holidays. Doesn't God work in amazing ways to nudge us? Here I was, weak and not able to do any of my normal household activities. But I could sit at my computer and write. During the first week of January, I began. The first order of business was finding a prayer team. I knew I couldn't tackle this without prayer, most especially prayer for my heart as I relived The Event to write about it. I emailed seven dear, godly women, and all seven women unhesitatingly agreed to be my team. I started to write.

Chapter 11

CHANGES IN RELATIONSHIPS

As we slogged along, somehow getting through one day at a time, dear friends continued to surround us. What we never anticipated, though, was that many of our relationships were about to change. When I went back to church after missing five weeks, Steve stayed home with my dad, a sacrifice he lovingly made for me, in part because he got out of the house every weekday for work. He wasn't feeling isolated as he knew I was. I got to see my grandchildren one day a week for a few hours, thanks to friends who sat with my dad, but otherwise, I wasn't able to leave the house. As much as I longed to be back at church, I also dreaded it. What if everyone descended on me? What if no one descended on me? What if I cried? God blessed my return, bringing just the right people who were quick to hug me and tell me they continued to pray for us. One person, after a long meaningful hug, talked about the deep grief she was still feeling from a miscarriage. I asked her if she had named her child. She gave a little gasp and said she had never thought about that, then pondered and proposed an unusual name and asked if I thought it could be for either a boy or a girl, since she didn't know which her child was. I thought it could, and I loved the name she had thought of! We both cried, standing there in the hallway with people casually moving past every now and then, oblivious to the remarkable moment that had just occurred. We cried for our losses, and I also cried in thankfulness that I actually helped someone else in their grief because of my own. I felt a glimmer of hope that God might use me, even in the dreadfulness of what I was going through, to help carry someone else along as they struggled under a heavy load.

Circle of Sorrow

At times, with tears too close to the surface, I couldn't bring myself to even look at others and didn't want anyone to stop me as I moved through the building. I looked down at the carpet, tilting my head towards the wall. Everyone respected my body language, probably with some relief that they didn't have to think of something to say. I understood that it's hard to know what to say. Even after Trevor left, I found myself saying to someone who had lost a loved one, "How are you doing?" And then immediately I apologized, saying, "I'm sorry, that was an awful question. You don't need to answer it again. Can I just give you a hug?" It's human nature to want to make a friend feel better, and it's natural to ask that obvious question. Until I experienced it myself, I never thought about how many people ask that same question and how hard it is for the grieving one. Steve and I talked about it and came up with ready answers. When the inevitable, well-intentioned question was asked, we responded with "Breathing in and breathing out," or "Taking it one day at a time," or "Being carried through by the prayers of many," or something of the kind. For most people, that was sufficient. Some people replied, "No, I mean how are you really doing? How can I pray for you better?" Those people were giving us permission to talk a little more. We didn't ever want to give people more to carry with us than they were meant to take on. We had done that during the initial weeks, and we regretted that we had given some of our visitors a load they weren't prepared to carry. At that point, our fog was so thick we had no concept of how our sharing might affect others, but now, with the fog slowly thinning, we felt the need to filter our grief and to confide more deeply only with those who truly wanted to hear more. For those who gently probed, not satisfied with our ready answers, we shared a little more.

I noticed that some people avoided me. One person admitted on my social media post at the six-month mark that he did tend to avoid me because he simply had no idea what to say to me. I appreciated his honesty! And as I said in the post, it's okay. I understand it's awkward. I respect that he didn't want to inadvertently cause me more pain. That person, a year later, made a beeline towards me in church one Sunday and started chatting about random things. It was clear to me that he was breaking the ice, wanting to be able to have normal conversations with me again. I hope he knows how much that meant to me. Others drifted away. I suspect they were unable to focus on anything other than our loss and it was easier just not to engage with me. Again, that was okay, though it made me sad. I began jumping on interactions with a quick focus on something about the other person. I needed people to know that I was still me, I still cared about them, I was still a safe person who would maintain confidences, and I wanted to continue to have a relationship with them. I was also a hurting person, and sometimes they might see that. I learned to be up front about my grief. If I was talking to someone and the tears started to surface, it could be a conversation stopper. I didn't want to make my friends uncomfortable, but I also needed to be honest. Grief isn't something we just get over after a set amount of time. Losing my child by his own hand will forever be a part of who I am now. There will always be a sadness just below the surface. It would be a lie to say otherwise. Some friends are close enough that they'll always carry that sadness right beside me, and I'm so grateful for them. But when that sadness breaks the surface in the midst of a conversation, it tends to make the other person feel awkward and uncertain about how to proceed. I'll tell whoever I'm talking to that it's okay, sometimes I need to cry and it will pass, usually mustering up at least a weak smile as I say those words. That's been helpful, relieving people of the necessity to try to find the right words to comfort me, and they're given permission to continue with the conversation without refocusing on my grief. This didn't happen overnight. It took time and prayer to reach that point, but the effort has been worth it as I've seen both close and casual friendships grow stronger.

Of course, some people will always be intimidated by our loss. They've chosen to take a step back. And that's okay. I wish it wasn't that way, but not everyone is able to figure out how to relate to us in our "new normal." Whenever they see us, their first thought is clearly of our loss, and it stymies them. Some are paralyzed by the fear that they'll make our grief worse. I learned this when someone admitted it to me. They won't. They aren't suddenly reminding us that we lost our son, as if we had somehow forgotten. For those people, if they ever experience first-hand what we've been through, we'll be at their sides. For now, we won't force relationships on those who are uncomfortable with us. God provides the community we need.

I haven't experienced anyone saying anything horrifically inappropriate, but others have. In my online grief group, one woman told us about a friend who had tried to comfort her by saying he had lost his dog and now he understood how she felt. Really? Comparing losing a child to losing a dog? In that group, with many who aren't believers, the responses varied from forgiving the person, knowing they were just trying to help, to advising to blast the person with profanity and cut him out of her life. I need much grace as I wade through my grief, sometimes unable to focus on a friend because I'm hurting too much, or perhaps preoccupied with some memory that popped into my mind. I also need to extend grace to others who think they're being helpful but aren't. I can appreciate their efforts even if they fall short. How could they know? They haven't been through this. They're trying, and that matters.

One person told me with a bright smile after several months, "Your eyes are starting to get their twinkle back!" I know she meant well, but to me it felt like she was saying, "You're finally getting over your loss! You don't miss him anymore! How wonderful!" I blinked and opened my mouth several times, but nothing came out. There was simply no response I could think of for that insensitive effort. I finally emitted a weak, "Thank you." Again, I've been shown much grace in times when I've tried to help and instead hurt. I need to extend the same. The same need to show grace applies to those who wished me a cheerful "Happy Mother's Day." They were people who knew I had lost a child. One wished me a happy Mother's Day as I was leaving church with tears streaming down my face. I choked a tearful "Thank you," to her, then wished her the same. Her face was puzzled, and she probably remembered seconds after I left. Yet I'm still a mother, and the sentiment was not wrong, just perhaps would have been better without the radiant smile.

I've found that my language has changed. There are words and phrases I avoid. I sent a message to a friend who might be traveling close by and almost told her to give me a call if she had time to kill. I typed the k, then backspaced. She could give me a call if she had time to spare. I don't like to use the word dead. That plant isn't dead. It's withered. My grandkids made up a game they call "dead man." One person has to keep their eyes closed and try to tag one of the others, who dodge loudly or stand silently. I call it "blind man," but my grandson insists that his name is better. That's fine, but I'll keep calling it blind man. If someone says that this outfit or that cake is "to die for," I cringe and think, "No, no it isn't!" In a conversation with a friend about a house decision she and her husband disagreed on, she laughed and said if he got his way, to just shoot her already. I think my eyes must have glazed over, but she didn't notice. And she didn't need to notice. I don't need the world to change to accommodate my grief. This is my journey, and I will learn how to deal with those things. In time, my vocabulary may shift back to using words I avoid right now, and perhaps it won't. Even my vocabulary is part of this grief journey.

Changes in Relationships

Steve struggled with being in church. Over a year later, he felt that people still looked at him with pity and knew that when he talked to them, they were thinking about Trevor and didn't know what to say to him. He shrank away from conversation with casual friends. He would talk to his close buddies, and he regularly started conversations with people he didn't know, which was something he had always done. But people he knew only casually were difficult for him. One day, he had a conversation with a dear man who had lost his wife to cancer only a month or so after our loss. He commented to Steve that he usually attends the 8:40 service. Steve immediately understood what he meant. The service starts at 8:30. By intentionally coming late, he avoided being inundated with well-meaning people with whom he wasn't ready to converse. As they talked, our friend recognized Steve's need and invited him to be part of his men's group. That group has helped to turn things around for Steve. The group is usually small, and the men in it are mature in their faith. Some have been through some extremely difficult times in the last years, so Steve doesn't feel like everyone is looking at him as "that poor guy." He's able to talk about his grief only if he wants to, and he's able to share in the pain others are experiencing. His inclusion in that group is a relief to my heart as he's enveloped by the love of strong men in the church.

Steve also discovered that volunteering for church events enables him to chat with the focus being automatically on the event rather than on him. Our church regularly does community outreach events and asks members to volunteer to help out. About a year and a half after losing Trevor, Steve offered to do whatever was needed at the annual Spring Festival. Hundreds of people from the surrounding neighborhoods come for the petting zoo, crafts, pony rides, a bounce house, and much more, and many hands are required to keep things running smoothly. Steve expected he would be given a neon vest and direct traffic for parking or point people to where the bathrooms are. Instead, he was assigned face painting. He dove into the task enthusiastically and with a bit of trepidation. He had never face painted before. His first customer was a five-year-old from our small group. He asked Steve for a teal snake. Steve successfully created a snake on the boy's face, which his mom texted to me. It was adorable! Another boy asked for a soccer ball. Steve, an avid baseball aficionado, pondered what a soccer ball looks like. He was pretty sure it has hexagons. He painted away, wondering if this customer would cringe at his efforts. The child loved it and came back later for a snake on the other cheek. Steve had lots of interaction with both kids and adults, and he relaxed. He found that volunteering was a natural way to be with others, and the event itself kept the focus from being on his loss, for both himself and for others.

In her book, *What Grieving People Wish You Knew About What Really Helps (and What Really Hurts)*, Nancy Guthrie related an incident in which a friend who had lost a child told her,

> "It wasn't so much what people said that hurt," she said. "What hurt was when people said nothing at all." All too soon I discovered what she meant; the silence that seemed to scream that my daughter's life didn't even merit a mention. And, oh, how it hurt.[40]

I think I would rather someone told me they now know how I feel because they recently lost their dog than for them to say nothing at all. But how much better it would be if people actually had some idea of what things are helpful to say and what things are hurtful. Nancy Guthrie goes into detail with thoughtful guidelines. Every person is different, and the relationship I have with someone is important to recognize. What a close friend says as opposed to a new acquaintance should be vastly different. Nancy elaborates on not assuming what the person is feeling, not comparing my pain and your pain, not rushing a conversation as if pushing the grieving person towards the best path for a fast journey, not making it about yourself instead of the grieving person, listening more than talking, not telling someone what they need to do (get more sleep, eat healthy food, etc.), and more. She also discusses the unhelpful things many people say. She writes,

> Grieving people often hear:
>
> Silly sentimental things such as, "I guess God just needed another angel in heaven."
>
> Can't-you-just-look-on-the-bright-side things such as, "Well, at least you can have other children."
>
> Sum-it-up-spiritually things such as, "It must have been God's plan."
>
> Twisted-scripture things such as, "You know that God will never give you more than you can handle."
>
> Outright-wrong-but-spiritual-sounding things such as, "God needed her with him more than we needed her here."
>
> Quazi[sic]-spiritual-but-ultimately-meaningless things such as, "I'm sending you good thoughts."

> Put-on-the-pressure things such as, "Just think about how God is going to use you because of what you've been through."[41]

I did hear some of those types of comments. One person said to me that my loved one was looking down from Heaven at me. That in and of itself wasn't a bad thing to say, except I knew that person was an atheist and that his comment meant nothing to him, and thus nothing to me. I asked him, pointedly but kindly, "What does that mean to you?" He stumbled for words and abruptly exited the conversation. Some relationships may flounder as people shy away from actually engaging with a deeply hurting person. That doesn't mean they weren't really friends after all, it just means that they aren't the ones who can cope with this wound. It's okay to move on. It's okay for your friend-set to change.

What I've learned is that saying something is generally better than saying nothing. A hug counts as saying something. With some thought ahead of time, I can come up with some things to say that won't overwhelm my friend. Questions like "How are you doing *today*?" or "How has your week been?" or "How can I pray for you over the next few days?" invite a response with as much or as little detail as a hurting friend wants to open up about in that moment. Friends have told me things like, "I don't know how you're feeling, but I want you to know that I'm continuing to pray for you." A few women have stopped to hug me and state, "Oh my dear friend, I'm so glad to see you today!" When someone I don't know very well calls me a dear friend, I know they've been praying for me. Praying for someone gives us a closeness that we might not have had otherwise. Recently, a friend texted me asking what I thought would be an appropriate way to reach out to a woman she didn't know well who had just lost her husband. She wanted to do or say something, but she wasn't sure if it would be welcome, since they didn't know each other well. She asked if texting scripture would be okay, or just telling her she was praying. I was so glad to be able to tell her my thoughts! Absolutely, text both scripture and that you're praying. And if you can, send a card. As I thought, it occurred to me, and I relayed to her, that after a month or a few, people tend to think that the loss isn't so much anymore and the support drifts away. But that woman is thinking about her lost husband every single day. I suggested putting a note on her calendar to remind herself to send another card on special days, such as the late husband's birthday, their anniversary, or holidays, or even for no special day at all. Cards that arrive long after the loss happened speak an especially deep love to a grieving person.

Circle of Sorrow

I've heard it said that in hard times you'll find out who your real friends are. While there may be some truth in that, I think that when you're traveling a long, rocky, wave-drenched road of grief, some people are simply better equipped to walk with you than others. I've learned to let go of those relationships in which someone isn't able to walk well with me. I'm not rejecting them or pushing them away. I'm just not requiring them to interact with a person they aren't equipped to interact with. Maybe at some point, those friendships will rekindle. Maybe not. For now, I'm clinging to what and who God brings me, treasuring the profound and genuine love of many. Some of them probably don't even know how impactful their sincerity has been. I thank God for every person He has used to help us in this journey.

Chapter 12

WORSHIP, HEAVEN, AND LOOKING AHEAD

Five weeks after Trevor left us, I returned to church. I sat in the sound booth, proofreading the PowerPoint during rehearsal. As I focused on the arrangements, looking at lyrics and listening to the singers, the lump in my throat grew so that it felt like a football. With only those involved in the worship service present, I was able to pray and reflect on being back at church without being overwhelmed. Many of those present came over after rehearsal to just give me a hug, which didn't help the football, but did help my heart. I cried with each hug, and everyone, even if they were uncomfortable, just hugged me tighter. Slowly, the 8:30 crowd trickled in. We in the sound booth tend to be a bit invisible, for which I was grateful. A few people noticed I was back and came over to hug me and tell me they were praying for us. I felt relief as the service started and no attention came my way, but my relief was abruptly replaced by dismay as the first worship song started. I don't have a lovely public singing voice, but I can carry a tune and love to sing, especially in church as my voice joins with scores of others to create what we hope is acceptable worship to our holy God. As I opened my mouth, the first word I sang broke the dam and tears flooded down my face. I listened as others sang, and I worshiped from my heart, but I couldn't sing. As each new song began, I attempted to gather myself to let my voice blend in with praises to my Savior, but each time, the tears gushed again, tears of deep grief. I wanted so much to sing, to find some temporary relief from my pain by immersing myself in worshipping my Lord, but worship somehow made me more acutely aware of my loss. I didn't understand. The following week, I was better prepared, knowing what might happen. My heart was ready, and I was strong. And the tears flowed again. Every week, I found myself unable to sing. A few times, I made it through three or four words, but then crumbled again. I asked Steve if he sang during worship, and he looked at me, a bit puzzled, answering, "Of course! It's the highlight of my week!" He mourned and prayed with me over not being able to sing, but it continued for weeks. I posted to my online group, directing my question to other believers. I asked if anyone else had experienced this. Many had, and they, like me, didn't understand it. They wanted desperately to participate in worship, but they too had that football-sized lump in their throats with tears just waiting to be released. The weeks turned into months, and still I couldn't sing. I worshipped deeply, just not out loud. The lyrics saturated my heart, ministering to me even as they made me cry. Grief is a very lonely thing, even with those who are grieving the same loss. Steve and I share our grief, yet both of us are also alone in it. No one can step right into your heart with you. As I contemplated the lyrics in front of me during worship, I felt an intense closeness to God, and along with that, an acute awareness that Trevor was worshipping now at His very feet. What a glorious thing, even as I wept and missed him. I worshipped through the lyrics, silently reflecting,

> He will hold me fast, He will hold me fast,
> For my Savior loves me so
> He will hold me fast.[42]

I felt physically held, as though I were wrapped tightly in God's arms, safe, protected, comforted in the storm. The lyrics often spoke my pain, so poetically and exactly, and I sat quietly reflecting on my God, who knows my heartache, who has carried me in my weakness, and who I know will continue to carry me without fail. We sang, others out loud and I silently,

> Dear Refuge of my weary soul,
> on Thee, when sorrows rise,
> on Thee, when waves of trouble roll,
> my fainting hope relies...
> Hast Thou not bid me seek Thy face?
> And shall I seek in vain?
> And can the ear of sov'reign grace
> be deaf when I complain?
> No, still the ear of sov'reign grace
> attends the mourner's prayer;

> O may I ever find a place
> to breath my sorrows there.⁴³

This old hymn was written by a woman who had suffered loss, chronic pain, and many other adversities. I heaved with sobs as I meditated on God's faithfulness, how He hears my cries, my pleas, attending to this mourning mother's prayers. This grief, so foreign and so despicable, drew me close to God with comfort, yet the worship magnified my pain. Grief is a strange thing. God met me with a special, intense awareness of His presence, yet even as I found deep solace in that, it also brought my grief back to the forefront as I reflected on why God was especially close to me in those moments.

Sometimes, just a single line tore at my heart. As we sang

> Ye who long pain and sorrow bear
> Praise God and on Him cast your care⁴⁴

I sat, pondering the lyrics and praying, "Oh Lord, hear my cries and help me bear this unending sorrow." How long would this weighty pain last, how long would my sorrow keep my voice from singing out as I longed to do? The lyrics became prayers, intense pleas to God to help us to endure the pain and to trust Him as we continued through this dark tunnel.

I lifted the lyrics in silent prayer as others lifted them in song. I sat in the sound booth, quietly weeping, Sunday after Sunday. Sometimes the music elicited sweet, tearful memories, like Reginald Heber's 1826 hymn, "Holy, Holy, Holy."⁴⁵ How many times did Trevor choose that for his bedtime song as a little boy? We must have sung that hymn hundreds of times as a family at his request. Or the day we sang a song that contained a scripture that Trevor especially loved. When Trevor graduated from high school, Zac asked each senior to share a favorite piece of scripture. Trevor shared 1 Corinthians 15:55, "O death, where is your victory? O death, where is your sting?" When those words came up in worship, they stabbed me with renewed heartache.

In the past, I've often sung alone at home in worship, but singing corporately engages my heart differently. The closeness to God when I'm alone is personal. Corporate worship, while still personal, is collective and offers up to God praises magnified by all of our individual voices joining together in exultation. I doubt that anyone else was thinking of my loss during their worship, but I felt the community of God's people singing with me as I grieved. With my internal voice, I sang passionately, emotionally,

Circle of Sorrow

> When through the deep waters I call thee to go,
> the rivers of sorrow shall not overflow;
> for I will be near thee, thy troubles to bless,
> and sanctify to thee thy deepest distress
> When through fiery trials thy pathway shall lie,
> my grace, all sufficient, shall be thy supply[46]

This raging river would not overtake us permanently. We would continue to find strength in Christ, one day at a time, and when that strength failed, we would rest in Him. We had been through the fire, and we would look for how God might refine us, drawing us closer to Him and helping us to reflect Him in our daily lives as we continued in this river of grief. I sang internally, with deep grief as well as profound thanksgiving.

My non-singing worship lasted for eight or nine months. Worship was sweet and earnest, but my outward expression was only through tears. Gradually, I was able to sing a few words at a time, then a few lines at a time, then a song at a time, and finally, instead of tears, my words poured out in a torrent of fervent praise. Elated, I sang, then cried with mingled joy and grief after the service because I hadn't cried during the exuberant songs that expressed my feelings better than my own words ever could. In hindsight, God used that time of not being able to sing to help me to focus even more intently on the lyrics of every song, almost ignoring the accompanying music. The strong, poetic, meaty lyrics ministered to my heart and helped me to grieve as I needed. I couldn't see that at the time. I just wanted to be "normal" again and sing as I always had. God gave me more than that. I don't think I'll ever sing quite like I used to. Not having been raised in the church, worship has always struck me deeply, since I experienced it for the first time as a young adult. Now it's deeper still. I had no idea that worship would become so beautifully intensified because of this traumatic journey. That special awareness of God's personal presence with me has slowly waned. I miss it. But I no longer need it like I did in the beginning. God blessed me with that intense closeness when I felt like I was drowning, enabling me to take the next breath. I thank God with tears for that gift, and, like Mary, I'll treasure it up in my heart.

I found myself thinking a lot about Heaven. I wanted to know more about the place where my son now lives. I dove into Randy Alcorn's book *Heaven*.[47] He's very clear that some of what he thinks are his own conclusions based on his searching the scriptures, and I always keep that in mind, but he's done the deep dive and supports what he says well. We don't know a lot about Heaven, a word I now capitalize because, as Randy Alcorn points out, it's a real place and should be capitalized as any proper noun is.[48] One day there will be a new Heaven and a new Earth, but for now, where are our loved ones dwelling? They're with God. We know that. But what is the current Heaven like? Are there streets of gold, and a river with fruit trees? Or are our loved ones floating aimlessly awaiting the final new Heaven?

Alcorn calls the current Heaven "the present or intermediate Heaven."[49] Until the new Heaven and new Earth are brought forth, our loved ones in Heaven are in an intermediate Heaven, not yet the final place where all who are covered by the blood of Christ will dwell eternally. He addresses the question that many have about whether our loved ones are in an unconscious state, waiting for the new Heaven to be formed. He points out, "Every reference in Revelation to human beings talking and worshiping in Heaven prior to the resurrection of the dead demonstrates that our spiritual beings are conscious, not sleeping, after death."[50]

But does my son have a body to walk around in? I wanted to know this. I wanted to picture him where he is now. Alcorn says that we really don't know. Many scholars have studied this and have come to opposite conclusions. Alcorn says what we do know is

> We do *not* receive resurrection bodies immediately after death. Resurrection is not one-at-a-time. If we have intermediate forms in the intermediate Heaven, they won't be our true bodies, which have died. Continuity is *only* between our original and resurrection bodies. *If* we are given intermediate forms, they are at best temporary vessels (comparable to the human-appearing bodies that angels sometimes take on), distinct from our true bodies, which remain dead until our resurrection.[51]

As I sat in my office chair reading what brilliant minds have spent years seeking to understand, I often had to quietly swivel around and lean back, silently gazing through the windows, simply pondering, perplexed by the things that are beyond knowing. R.C. Sproul says

> Historically, classical Christian theology speaks of what we call the *status intermedius*, or the intermediate state. That has to do with where we go immediately upon death, as distinguished from our state after the final resurrection. This is what the New Testament indicates when Paul says that it was more needful for him to stay here for us, but to depart and be with Christ would be far better (Phil. 1:23–24). He indicates that, as soon as we die, our souls go immediately into the presence of Christ. In the intermediate state,

however, we are disembodied souls. We won't have our glorified bodies until after the coming of Christ and the great resurrection. At that point, our souls will be reunited with our bodies.[52]

Maybe Trevor has a temporary body for his soul to reside in while he waits for the new Heaven, the final place where he'll receive his resurrected body. Maybe he doesn't. Probably he doesn't. But he's still him, he still has his own distinct personality, his wit, his gifts, but with no sin. I can accept that I'm not able to know what God has hidden from us, returning again to Deuteronomy 29:29, that God's mysteries aren't meant for us to understand yet. I've read books and internet articles, listened to podcasts, and watched videos trying to ascertain what exactly the intermediate Heaven is like. There are people who say they've been there during near-death experiences. Can we trust their accounts?

In *Imagine Heaven*, John Burke tells how he initially wrote off accounts of near-death experiences. But as he studied scripture and read personal stories, he "started to see the difference between what they *reported* experiencing and the *interpretation* they might give to that experience" (emphasis his).[53] Burke slowly became convinced that because of the similarity of the actual reported experiences, as opposed to what assumptions or conclusions anyone might have come to, near-death experiences are worth considering. He detailed stories of people blind from birth who described visual details after their near-death experiences, as well as children who had not been exposed to stories of others' experiences, yet their descriptions matched. Burke combed through thousands of accounts of moving through a tunnel, seeing a bright light, and being approached by a figure gleaming with light who they instinctively knew loved them. All the beings seen shone with light, but there was One whose light was far greater, brighter than any light any of these near-death people had ever seen on Earth, yet it didn't hurt their eyes to look directly at it. Some people said they saw colors they had never seen on Earth. Many people said their experiences of Heaven couldn't be expressed with any known words. This fits with what Paul says in 2 Corinthians 12:2–4. He talks about being caught up to the third Heaven. He declares in verse 4 that "he heard things that cannot be told, which man may not utter." Yet Randy Alcorn writes,

> Too often, people view accounts of visiting Heaven as gospel. Obviously, God can show someone the afterlife if he so chooses. But "it is appointed for man to die once" (Hebrews 9:27). Since these stories are told by people who will 'die twice,' it seems likely

that they did not truly die the first time, even if vital signs weren't measurable. A person's memories under heavy sedation—and his or her ability to distinguish dreams from reality—aren't reliable, but God's word is (John 17:17).[54]

Burke obviously respects Alcorn's work, quoting him a number of times to support his own thoughts, yet these two well-researched authors reached opposite conclusions. How do we reconcile that? Ultimately, I have to say we don't know, and we can't on this side of Heaven. But I wonder whether near-death experiences are to our modern American culture what signs and wonders were in Old Testament times.

There are things too wonderful for us to know, and there are things that are beyond what we can comprehend even if someone who had actually experienced them could adequately describe them. I have grown to accept the not-knowing with contentment because I know that however Trevor's existence is right now, it's far better than what he left behind, and he has a glimpse of the final Heaven that is far clearer than any of us stuck here on this current Earth can possibly have. Still, I wanted to envision what he might be doing, who he might be talking to, how he might be worshipping. Greg Laurie pulled together many scriptures in his two-part sermon entitled, "Let's Talk About Heaven." He says,

> Well, we know we will be worshiping, and that's, of course, why I exist, to bring glory to God, but Revelation 15 says, I saw a glass sea mixed with fire, and there stood all the people who had been victorious over the Beast, that would be the Antichrist, and his image, and the number representing his name. They were holding harps, so there are harps in heaven that God had given them, and they were singing the song of Moses, the servant of God, and the song of the Lamb. So there will be singing in heaven, and I think, one of the reasons for the unbridled worship in heaven is because now we know all things. All of our questions are answered. All of our pain is removed, all of our tears are dried.[55]

Is Trevor already worshipping with musical instruments before God? I don't know, but I don't think it's wrong to imagine and hope that he is. What are musical instruments in Heaven like? We don't know, other than trumpets and harps, but I dream that there are instruments breathtakingly magnificent creating melodies that would defy earthly description. Greg Laurie goes on to describe the wedding supper of the Lamb and how glorious the food in Heaven will be. He brings out Matthew 8:11, in which we're told we'll take our place at the feast with Abraham, Isaac, and Jacob. Is Trevor dining on heavenly delicacies while shooting the breeze with the heroes of the faith? Do our loved ones know what's going on here on Earth? Greg Laurie says they probably do, but with perspective. We know that scripture says there's rejoicing in Heaven when someone comes to Christ. Laurie says,

> Then Jesus tells the story of the prodigal son, and how that boy came back to his father again, and then he says, 'Likewise, I tell you, 'there's more joy in the presence of the angels of God 'over one sinner who repents'. Now, we read that and think, well, that means the angels rejoice every time a sinner repents. Yeah, they probably do, but Jesus did not say, there is joy among the angels, rather, He said that when a sinner repents, there's joy in the presence of the angels of God.
>
> So I think they're rejoicing, too, but maybe we're rejoicing. Maybe in heaven, you're aware that someone you had prayed for for your entire life on earth, just came to Christ, and you're aware of their salvation, and you're giving God glory for that. So there is an awareness in heaven of what is happening on earth.[56]

So perhaps Trevor sees what his parents are going through, our heartache and ongoing grief. But if he does, he has a different perspective, and it's not with sadness or regret. Maybe, as John Piper speculates,[57] Trevor is now part of the great cloud of witnesses, rooting for us to keep staying strong in our faith, to finish our own races well.

I love what Greg Laurie says from Colossians 3:2,

> We are to set our hearts, and we are to set our minds on things above. This phrase set your mind can be translated think. Or more thoroughly have this inner disposition. Lemme put it another way. The verse is actually saying simply think Heaven, think Heaven. That's something we're all supposed to do as Christians. And by the way the verb that's used in this verse is in the present tense so it can be translated keep thinking Heaven, or keep thinking about Heaven, or keep seeking Heaven. Put it all together it's a constantly be seeking and thinking about Heaven.[58]

When life seems smooth, it's easy to forget to ponder what Heaven is like. When I was thrown into more than I could possibly handle, stopping and focusing my mind on Heaven, on who created it and who dwells there, enabled me to breathe and to trust that God would keep His promise to never leave or forsake me, and He has kept that promise. I find peace, contentment, and joy as I reflect on what I know about Heaven. I'm sad much of the time, but I still have joy, a fruit of the spirit, not to be confused with happiness, which is an emotion. And it's a deeper joy than in the past. In his book, *Walking with God Through Pain and Suffering*, Dr. Timothy Keller says,

> . . .we must not define *rejoicing* as something that precludes feelings of grief, or doubt, weakness, and pain. Rejoicing in suffering happens *within* sorrow. . . .It doesn't come after the sorrow. It doesn't come after the uncontrollable weeping. The weeping drives you into the joy, it enhances the joy, and then the joy enables you to actually feel your grief without its sinking you.[59]

I've grown to dislike the term "moving on" in grief. It conveys to me that staying where I am is wrong. But grief has no timeline. I can't and shouldn't rush it. Most of us are familiar with the concept of stages of grief, if not the actual lists developed. The first list, created by Dr. Elisabeth Kübler-Ross, identified five stages, including denial, anger, bargaining, depression, and acceptance. A more recent list adds an upward turn and a working through or reconstruction.[60] I recall several months after The Event sitting with friends who had lost two children and telling them, puzzled, that I had no anger. Others had assured me that I would and that I would need to work through it. Was I not grieving correctly? What was I doing wrong that I wasn't going through all the stages of grief? These dear friends told me that neither of them had experienced anger, either. They helped me to understand that we may go through all of those stages, but we may not. We may move through them in order, or we may move back and forth. For those who do experience that anger, especially at God, I think the way through that is to dive deeply into what they know about Him, focusing on who He is, how powerful and wise He is, how dearly He loves His children, and what eternity with Him will look like. He has the bigger picture, which we can't possibly comprehend from where we sit. It will most likely take significant time and prayer to work through that anger, but God is unchanging. He'll carry you through faithfully as you cry out to Him.

I will grow and change with time, but no one, not even I, can predict what today or next week or next year will be like in this journey. I'm different now. Everything is different now. Steve and I measure time as before The Event and after The Event. Pondering Heaven has helped me to grow in faith and in my knowledge of God, and I'm learning the hard, complicated role of being a mother who has lost a child to suicide. But what caught me

Circle of Sorrow

by surprise was a slow change that happened in my heart as I thought about where Trevor now is.

Our senior pastor, Steve Constable, participated in a short-term mission trip to Uganda in 2023. One of the prayer updates from another team member spoke of a devotional that Steve led from Psalm 126. He talked about how when we come to worship, we should be bringing our hard things with us, not laying them to the side. We need to bring everything before Him when we come to worship. I thought about that. I had, of course, been bringing my hard things with me in every quiet time, every prayer, every worship time. As I thought of Steve (Constable, not Wozny) sharing that devotion in Africa, though, my thoughts drifted across the globe. In parts of Africa, babies aren't given a name until they're at least a year old because the death rate is so high. During war time, babies and small children have been ripped from their mothers' arms and killed or taken captive to be raised as child soldiers. In China, up until 2016, baby girls were left out in fields to die because parents were allowed only one child, and generally preferred a boy. In my own sphere, my Circle of Sorrow has grown to fifteen other families who have lost a child. How all of those parents, here and across the globe, must ache! I thought about Steve's devotion and over the course of a week or so realized I had moved into a new stage in my grief process. As my husband and I sat in our glider rockers debriefing our days one evening, I told him that I felt that I was understanding our life journeys with God better, and that our suffering is not unique. He looked at me strangely, and he gently, quietly, disagreed. But as I continued, he got an ah-ha moment. So many, many people have experienced this grief, the grief of losing a child. We think we shouldn't suffer in this life. But we do, and we will, and what we personally suffer is not more than people in other countries experience every single day. I think a lot more about eternity, and when I do, I'm no longer thinking that when I get to Heaven, Trevor will be there. I'm thinking, "Jesus will be there, and I'll see Him face to face! And Trevor will be there, too!" Nearer, my God, to Thee.[61]

I think back to that day when Steve grabbed those two sodas and headed out to the deck with our youngest. How hopeful we were! At last, this prodigal had returned! Then our world turned inside out and upside down. It seems like last week and a hundred years ago. We still hurt, some days more intensely than others. I think we always will. Memories pop into our minds with the smallest reminders. One day I was putting some clean towels away in the linen closet outside Trevor's old room. I remembered the time when he was around twenty-five and I was putting things into that linen closet one evening when I heard an odd noise from behind Trevor's door. He wasn't home, so I opened his door to look for the source of the noise. There in his room was a five-foot-high metal cage holding two huge white rats. Those things were enormous, the size of guinea pigs! Within seconds I was calling his phone. He answered with a hello, then I streamed out with non-stop angst, "There are rats in my house, why are there rats in my house, you have rats, why are there rats, WHY ARE THERE RATS IN MY HOUSE?" He burst into his chuckle-laugh and couldn't stop. Eventually I had to just hang up. I take the grandkids to Chick–fil–A occasionally, and I remember how the assistant manager, when I arrived to pick up my fourteen-year-old, allowed to work limited hours in Virginia, always raved about what a good worker he was, how he never just stood behind the register if it wasn't busy. He'd wipe down counters and refill condiments without being told, intent on being the best employee he could. Every time I see a red Jeep, I remember his first car. He informed me that another teenager at church was going to teach him to drive stick. I knew that young man, and he was a bit reckless in my opinion and had a questionable driving record. I put the ka-bosh on that and told him I would teach him. What I didn't tell him was that I hadn't driven a stick in over twenty years, and then it was in a borrowed car with a quick lesson, just enough to get me where I needed to be. I found videos online to refresh myself and successfully taught him, relating shifting gears to music, how he could feel the change in the engine when it was time to shift. I faked confidence pretty well, and he never realized that I was sweating profusely, hoping I wouldn't reveal my lack of experience. Someone in my "Buy Nothing" group posted a picture of a pile of teddy bears she wanted to give away. Instantly my mind went back to Trevor's beloved pile of teddy bears. I remembered when he asked me to make a suit for Nosey. He helped choose the fabric, and I made pants, a jacket, and a necktie for his teddy bear. For over a year, I often saw some small thing that I thought Trevor would like and moved to send him a text, remembering within a second or two that I couldn't. He would love to see his rescue cat so happy. I'd send him a quick pic of her, I thought. No, I wouldn't. His plants look so healthy. He'd love to see this one. I'd send him a pic. No, I wouldn't. Those moments of thinking I'll send him a text have waned, but the memories of his growing up are frequent and treasured. Some memories make me cry, some make me smile, but all are welcome. All are part of the grief journey.

We meet new people, and I'm conscious that they don't know. Steve and I had the same experience on the same day at church, one we hadn't talked about but were both dreading. As I walked across the sanctuary towards the sound booth between services, I noticed a young woman sitting alone with no one else nearby. I stopped to greet her and ask her if she was visiting. She had moved to Richmond and come to Stony Point Church in the same month as The Event. We chatted about the usual things people bring up with someone they don't know. I learned about her job, and then she asked if I have children. I told her that yes, I have three. I will never say I only have two. She asked if they're local, and I told her that only my daughter is local and elaborated on what town she was in and that she was the mother to my two grandchildren. Of course, she followed that up with, "And where do your sons live?" I mentally took a deep breath and answered that I have a son in Denver and one in Heaven. I had said it! I said it out loud and didn't cry! To her credit, she continued on with, "Oh, what does your son in Denver do?" She could have said, "I'm sorry for your loss," and that would have been wonderful, but I'm sure she was trying to figure out how to respond to that unexpected location and I don't fault her at all. I doubt I would have had the composure she had if someone had said that to me. Steve had the same experience with another new person that day, and he, too, said he has three children.

A little over a year after The Event, a dear friend, Laurie, and her mom, to whom I'm close enough that I call her Mom P., were going to be near Richmond. We found a location between where they would be and where I was and met for a lovely lunch together. I hadn't seen them in years. Their whole family was instrumental in my coming to the Lord, and Mom P. made my wedding dress for me. As we talked, I shared some of Trevor's story. Mom P. listened, then said quietly, "What if he was right? What if those two vehicles really were a gang?" I had abandoned that thought a few months after it all happened, concluding that it was Trevor's mental illness, not a real threat, that had escalated The Event. But Mom P. was right, and I was shaken. Maybe Trevor really did save us from a violent and painful death. There was some truth in the things that Trevor had feared. We know that for certain. I had to ponder that again, and I realized I needed to accept that we won't know the complete truth about those vehicles on this side of Heaven. There will always be unknowns. I have no choice in that, but I do have the choice to direct my thoughts to the Lord, to His word and His promises, and to rest in Him, continually. I will be still and know that He is God. (Psalm 46:10)

On most days now, my river is still flowing quickly, but there aren't usually rapids, though they do come occasionally. I long for calm waters where I can close my eyes and drift gently, but those days are rare. Maybe one day they'll be the norm. In the meantime, I'm hanging tightly to my raft, my lifeboat that is Jesus, my Anchor safe and secure.

> God's voice speaks deeper than what hurts,
> brighter than what is dark,
> more enduring than what is lost,
> truer than what has happened.
> David Powlison[62]

EPILOGUE

The journey of grief doesn't simply end. God will be using what He has allowed for us throughout the rest of our lives. I got a text from one of the women on my prayer team one day early in the spring of 2024. She had noticed in one of our local library branches that an event was planned for writing while working through grief. Knowing I was writing already, she thought I might be interested. I was, and the day signups opened, I was enrolled within five minutes.

When the day arrived, I was actually feeling a little resistant to going. I wondered if I would gain anything from it. Maybe it would help me as I continue to process grief. Maybe it would help me with writing this book. Maybe there was some other reason for me to be there. But I simply didn't want to go. It might be painful, and I'd had enough of pain. I started my car and prayed that God would help me to be open to whatever I should learn from it. Spoiler alert: I was absolutely supposed to be there!

There were seven women there, including the leader, a young widow. The leader and the young woman next to me were in their early 40s, and all the others were in my age range with adult children and grandchildren. We made introductions, with sharing optional. Four of us had lost children. When I spoke, I didn't think I would cry, but of course, I did. Some of those who lost a child didn't tell how. I did, briefly, and placed my hand on my Psalms journal, which I had brought for whatever writing we might do, and said that my faith was very important to me and that I had done quite a bit of journaling in that precious book.

One woman said she wanted to go last, but she jumped in before the quiet young woman next to me had a turn. She is in what she called "anticipatory grief," as her husband is dealing with cancer and is still going through treatment. She was the talker in the group. I turned to the woman next to me after the talker finished and asked her quietly, "Did you want to share?" The leader was on my other side and could hear. I'm sure she wouldn't have left that woman out, but I felt she had been overlooked and she had had tears on her face for the whole introduction time. She nodded, then told us she had lost her mom, that today was her mom's birthday, and that as the oldest daughter, all the planning had fallen to her, and she had had to be strong for the rest of her family. As she started, with the tears coming faster, I asked her if I could hug her, and she nodded. I scooted my chair over and hugged her for a few minutes as she talked, and I could feel the tension in her shoulder. If it were someone I knew, I would have kept hugging her, but after what seemed like the appropriate amount of time, I lowered my arm, then reached into my purse for tissues, which she gratefully accepted.

Now I can get to why I was at that event. We had twenty minutes left at the end, and the leader asked if we wanted to do another writing exercise or not. The talker spoke up and said, "I have a question for you," as she pointed at me. Everyone was a bit surprised at that, including me, but I nodded and said, "Okay." She said that I had mentioned that my faith was important to me. With an anguished face, she asked me how I deal with being angry at God. Being a talker, it took her a good minute or so to finish asking her question, giving me time to quickly pray. I told her that the stages of grief most of us have come to know were never meant to be used as they are. They were originally written as stages of accepting death for those with terminal illnesses.[63] Gradually, they became accepted as stages of grief. But they were never meant to be a chart that we go through, bing bing bing, now we're done. Some will go through all the stages, some won't, and we may go back and forth, in and out of them. I told her that I had never had anger towards God. Sin is in the world, and we all experience the effects of it, both our own and the sins of others. God didn't cause my son's death, sin did, and He can actually use horrendous things like that for good down the road. I told how Trevor had come to us in distress and blurted out, "Dad, I don't want to go to hell," and then I got to share the gospel, telling how Steve led Trevor back to the Lord! Clearly, shared the gospel! I heard the leader make a little noise like it was time for me to stop, but I ignored her. I had been asked a direct question, and one which many people struggle with, whether believers or not, and I wasn't going to stop. The leader let me continue without interrupting. I talked about how we can deal with being angry at God by remembering what we know about Him, who He is. He's all-powerful, and completely loving, and He isn't constrained by time and space like we are. He has the bigger picture. Because of the sacrifice of Christ to pay for our sins, death doesn't win. I spoke for at least five minutes, and as I finished, it was clear to me that this was why I was there. She had said she goes to a supper at a sister church to mine on Thursday evenings. I confirmed with her, "That's so-and-so's church, isn't it?" She was surprised that I knew who that pastor was—but being a sister church, the two pastors have swapped pulpits a few times, so I had met him. As we walked out afterward, she and I turned toward the same parking area while everyone else went the other direction. She told me that she doesn't go to that church, she just likes the supper and ignores the "Jesus talk" at the end. But I told her that her question was an important one and a good one to ask the pastor. I hope she'll actually talk to him!

There's one more thing. As we all gathered our belongings to leave, the young woman next to me hugged me and cried again, then said, "You have such peace!" She worried that she was grieving "wrong." I assured her that she wasn't, that grief is different for everyone, and it can't be rushed. We got to talk about that for several minutes. I didn't have an opening into sharing anything more about the Lord or the reason for my peace, but I trust that God can use whatever I said in His wise and powerful ways. Maybe she's just as much a reason as the talker was for me to be there. I hope she quietly ponders what she heard and pursues that peace by seeking the Lord.

Praise God! What an honor to have gotten to share His gospel with hurting people! Me! He used insignificant little non-eloquent me! Sometimes, He uses unexpected people. It's not something I'm seeking, but I'm open and will do my best to seize whatever opportunities our gracious God allows me.

Praise God from whom all blessings flow!

POSTSCRIPT

Two and a half years after our world turned sideways, I ran into a friend at church who had undergone a hip replacement and asked him how his healing was going, as I had been praying for him. He replied he was doing great, had no pain, and could even ride a bike. He joyfully urged me to put someone else on my prayer list in place of him. Standing there in a quiet corner of the sanctuary, we continued to chat, and I told him he and his wife are in another part of my regular prayers, for those who have lost a child, and they would always be part of that group. He expressed deep thanks for that, and I sensed it would be okay to ask a question I was reflecting on. I was only two and a half years in. I asked him what it's like now for him, almost thirty years later. His face transformed as he tenderly described his precious infant daughter, Kate, struggling with medical issues, and how she didn't survive a surgical procedure. His entire countenance looked gentle and peaceful as he reminisced about her, yet tears trickled down his face. Thirty years later, it's different, he said, but it still hurts. He misses her every day. We talked for quite some time, sharing that odd combination of grief and joy, something foreign to anyone who hasn't actually experienced it.

This is the road that God has given us, we who are in the Circle of Sorrow. We are in the Circle forever. There is no such thing as "This too shall pass," which is not scriptural. *This will not pass.* This is a part of us now and always will be. I relate to this scripture, the account of Elijah, running from the wrath of Jezebel:

> Elijah was afraid and ran for his life. When he came to Beersheba in Judah, he left his servant there, while he himself went a day's journey into the wilderness. He came to a broom bush, sat down under it and prayed that he might die. "I have had enough, Lord," he said. "Take my life; I am no better than my ancestors." Then he lay down under the bush and fell asleep.

Circle of Sorrow

> All at once an angel touched him and said, "Get up and eat." He looked around, and there by his head was some bread baked over hot coals, and a jar of water. He ate and drank and then lay down again.
>
> The angel of the Lord came back a second time and touched him and said, "Get up and eat, for the journey is too much for you." So he got up and ate and drank. Strengthened by that food, he traveled forty days and forty nights until he reached Horeb, the mountain of God. There he went into a cave and spent the night. (1 Kings 19:3–9)

This journey is too much for us. This passage poignantly illustrates how God carries us daily when we're weak and have no strength to go on. We may want to collapse and hide, but He hears us when we cry out to Him.

> The cords of death entangled me;
> the torrents of destruction overwhelmed me.
> The cords of the grave coiled around me;
> the snares of death confronted me.
> In my distress I called to the Lord;
> I cried to my God for help.
> From his temple he heard my voice;
> my cry came before him, into his ears. (Psalm 18:4–6)

God sees, He hears, He provides, and we find rest for our bodies and our souls. The Circle of Sorrow is held in the much larger circle of the hands of Jesus, He who knows grief. He holds us in His powerful and able grip.

ENDNOTES

1. David Huffstutler, "Ever Sing for Joy," The Fog of Grief, 09/03/2022, https://eversingingforjoy.blogspot.com/2022/09/the-fog-of-grief.html.
2. Jill Cohen, "Avoid Major Decision-Making While Grieving—Why This Is so Important," https://www.jillgriefcounselor.com/blog/avoid-decision-making-while-grieving?rq=moving.
3. Kirsten Schuder, "The Most Stressful Life Events in Order," Love to Know, 10/15/2022, https://www.lovetoknow.com/life/wellness/what-are-most-stressful-life-events.
4. Timothy Keller, *Walking with God through Pain and Suffering* (Dutton, 2013), 291.
5. C. S. Lewis, *A Grief Observed* (Bantam, 1976), 4.
6. C. S. Lewis, *A Grief Observed* (Bantam, 1976), 80.
7. C. S. Lewis, *A Grief Observed* (Bantam, 1976), 67.
8. David Powlison, *Grieving a Suicide: Help for the Aftershock*, Christian Counseling and Educational Foundation (New Growth Press, 2010), 17.
9. Czarina Ong, "Suicide not an unforgivable sin, says Rick Warren's wife whose son took his own life," *Christianity Today*, 09/18/2015, https://www.christiantoday.com/article/suicide-not-an-unforgivable-sin-says-rick-warrens-wife-whose-son-took-his-own-life/65021.htm#google_vignette.
10. Excerpt taken from *Understanding Heaven Passport*, copyright ©2013 by Insight for Living. All rights reserved worldwide. Used by permission. www.insight.org.
11. Survivors of Suicide Loss, "Dealing with Guilt After a Suicide," Survivors of Suicide Loss, 08/11/2021, https://www.sosmadison.com/blog/dealing-with-guilt-after-suicide.
12. Stacey Freedenthal, "'If Only': Self-Blame After a Loved One's Suicide," Speaking of Suicide: A site for suicidal individuals, loved ones, survivors, & others who care, 05/07/2014, https://speakingofsuicide.com/2014/05/07/if-only/.
13. Stacey Freedenthal, "'If Only': Self-Blame After a Loved One's Suicide," Speaking of Suicide: A site for suicidal individuals, loved ones, survivors, & others who care, 05/07/2014, https://speakingofsuicide.com/2014/05/07/if-only/.
14. GriefShare, Church Initiative, 4th ed., 2022 (note that the accompanying videos were updated in 2024 and the reference to suicide has been removed).
15. Robert Fleischmann, Jeffrey Samelson, and Christa Potratz, hosts, "Interview with Pastor Kurt Ebert on Suicide and Grief," *The Life Challenges Podcast*, 02/22/2022, https://www.buzzsprout.com/1792019/episodes/10121786-episode-24-interview-with-pastor-kurt-ebert-on-suicide-and-grief.
16. Centers for Disease Control and Prevention, "Leading Causes of Death," https://wisqars.cdc.gov/lcd/?o=LCD&y1=2021&y2=2021&ct=12&cc=ALL&g=00&s=0&r=0&r

Endnotes

y=0&e=0&ar=lcd1age&at=groups&ag=lcd1age&a1=0&a2=199.

17. Cleveland Clinic: Health Essentials, "Why Do We Cry? The Truth Behind Your Tears," 02/20/2022, https://health.clevelandclinic.org/tears-why-we-cry-and-more-infographic.

18. Cornerstone Hospice, "Physical Symptoms of Grief," https://cornerstonehospice.org/2141-2/.

19. American Heart Association, "Is Broken Heart Syndrome Real?," https://www.heart.org/en/health-topics/cardiomyopathy/what-is-cardiomyopathy-in-adults/is-broken-heart-syndrome-real.

20. Stephanie Hairston, "How Grief Shows Up in Your Body," WebMD, 07/11/2019, https://www.webmd.com/special-reports/grief-stages/20190711/how-grief-affects-your-body-and-mind.

21. Universität Ulm, "Chronic Stress Is Bad for Broken Bones: How Psychological Stress Impairs Bone Growth and Fracture Healing," Medical Xpress, 07/13/2023, https://medicalxpress.com/news/2023-07-chronic-stress-bad-broken-bones.html#google_vignette.

22. Nuala Mcbride, "Grief's Impact on Gut Health," The Nutritious Way, 12/13/2023, https://thenutritiousway.net/grief-nutrition/.

23. Johns Hopkins Medicine, "Depression and Suicide," https://www.hopkinsmedicine.org/health/conditions-and-diseases/depression-and-suicide.

24. Norwich City Football Club, YouTube Video, 10/10/2023, https://www.youtube.com/watch?v=tX8TgVR33KM.

25. Medically reviewed by: Christina M. Cammarata, PhD, Nemours Children's. Health: TeensHealth: Suicide, 04/2023, https://kidshealth.org/en/teens/suicide.html.

26. Amanda McMillan, "4 Possible Reasons Why Mental Health Is Getting Worse," Health.com, 08/21/2023, https://www.health.com/condition/depression/8-million-americans-psychological-distress.

27. American Psychological Association, "Mental Health Issues Increased Significantly in Young Adults Over Last Decade," 03/14/2019, https://www.apa.org/news/press/releases/2019/03/mental-health-adults.

28. Gonzalo Martinez-Ales, Daniel Hernandez-Calle, Nicole Khauli, and Katherine M. Keyes, "Why Are Suicide Rates Increasing in the United States? Towards a Multilevel Reimagination of Suicide Prevention," National Institutes of Health, 08/30/2020, https://www.ncbi.nlm.nih.gov/pmc/articles/PMC8699163/.

29. David Powlison, *God's Grace in Your Suffering* (Crossway, 2018), 62.

30. https://www.caritasva.org/.

31. John Piper, "Can Loved Ones in Heaven Look Down on Me?," desiring GOD, Episode 995, 01/27/2017, https://www.desiringgod.org/interviews/can-loved-ones-in-heaven-look-down-on-me.

32. John Piper, "Can Loved Ones in Heaven Look Down on Me?," desiring GOD, Episode 995, 01/27/2017, https://www.desiringgod.org/interviews/can-loved-ones-in-heaven-look-down-on-me.

33. Katie Polski, "Christian Living: Yes, a Loved One Is Watching from Heaven," The *Gospel Coalition*, 03/24/2023, https://www.thegospelcoalition.org/article/loved-one-watching-heaven/.

34. Tim Challies, "Does Nick Send Me Signs?," Challies, 11/04/2022, https://www.challies.com/articles/does-nick-send-me-signs/.

35. Austin DeArmond, "Grief: False Comforts for the Bereaved," Austin's Blog, 04/11/2023, https://austind90.wordpress.com/2023/04/11/false-comforts-for-the-bereaved/.

Endnotes

36. Thomas Chisholm, "Great Is Thy Faithfulness," 1923.
37. Tim Challies, "Does Nick Send Me Signs?," Challies, 11/04/2022, https://www.challies.com/articles/does-nick-send-me-signs/.
38. Reginald Heber, "Holy, Holy, Holy," 1826.
39. Horatio Spafford, "It Is Well," 1873.
40. Nancy Guthrie, *What Grieving People Wish You Knew About What Really Helps (and What Really Hurts)* (Crossway, 2016), 20.
41. Nancy Guthrie, *What Grieving People Wish You Knew About What Really Helps (and What Really Hurts)* (Crossway, 2016), 39.
42. Ada R. Habershon, "He Will Hold Me Fast," 1906.
43. Anna Steele, "The Soul's Only Refuge," 1760.
44. Paraphraser: William H. Draper; Author: St. Francis of Assisi, "All Creatures of Our God and King," 1225.
45. Reginald Heber, "Holy, Holy, Holy," 1826.
46. R. Keen and George Keith, "How Firm a Foundation," 1787.
47. Randy Alcorn, *Heaven* (Tyndale House, 2004).
48. Randy Alcorn, *Heaven* (Tyndale House, 2004), xix.
49. Randy Alcorn, *Heaven* (Tyndale House, 2004), 42.
50. Randy Alcorn, *Heaven* (Tyndale House, 2004), 47.
51. Randy Alcorn, *Heaven* (Tyndale House, 2004), 59.
52. R. C. Sproul, "Theology: Last Things: Heaven and Hell: Do Christians Go Immediately to Heaven When They Die?," Ligonier Ministries, https://www.ligonier.org/learn/qas/do-christians-go-immediately-to-heaven-when-they-die.
53. John Burke, *Imagine Heaven* (Baker, 2015), 16.
54. Randy Alcorn, "Let Go of Lies About Heaven: Eight Myths Many Believe," desiringGOD, 06/05/2020, https://www.desiringgod.org/articles/let-go-of-lies-about-heaven.
55. Greg Laurie, "Let's Talk About Heaven," Sermons.Love, https://sermons.love/greg-laurie/2482-greg-laurie-lets-talk-about-heaven.html.
56. Greg Laurie, "Let's Talk About Heaven," Sermons.Love, https://sermons.love/greg-laurie/2482-greg-laurie-lets-talk-about-heaven.html.
57. John Piper, "Can Loved Ones in Heaven Look Down on Me?," desiring GOD, Episode 995, 01/27/2017, https://www.desiringgod.org/interviews/can-loved-ones-in-heaven-look-down-on-me.
58. Greg Laurie, "Let's Talk About Heaven," Sermons.Love, https://sermons.love/greg-laurie/2482-greg-laurie-lets-talk-about-heaven.html.
59. John Piper, "Can Loved Ones in Heaven Look Down on Me?," desiring GOD, Episode 995, 01/27/2017, https://www.desiringgod.org/interviews/can-loved-ones-in-heaven-look-down-on-me.
60. Timothy Keller, *Walking with God through Pain and Suffering* (Dutton, 2013), 253.
61. Kimberly Holland, "The Stages of Grief and What to Expect," Healthline, 05/17/2023, https://www.healthline.com/health/stages-of-grief#7-stages.
62. Sarah Flowers Adams, "Nearer, My God, to Thee," 1841.
63. Russell Friedman, "Stages of Grief: The Myth," The Grief Recovery Method, 01/21/2020, https://www.griefrecoverymethod.com/blog/2012/01/stages-grief-myth.

www.ingramcontent.com/pod-product-compliance
Lightning Source LLC
Chambersburg PA
CBHW071211160426
43196CB00011B/2254